The Fun Guide to Disneyland For Kids!

2024

© 2022-2024 Travel Made Easy. All rights reserved.

Here you leave today—and visit the worlds of yesterday, tomorrow, and fantasy.

- Walt Disney

Copyright © Travel Made Easy 2022-2024

Visit us at www.TravelMadeEasy.co.

All Rights Reserved. No part of this book may be reproduced or transmitted in any form by any means, electronic or mechanical, including photocopying, scanning or recording, or by any information storage and retrieval system, except as may be expressly permitted under Sections 107 or 108 of the 1976 Copyright Act or by the publisher. Reviewers may quote brief passages in a critical article or review to be printed in a magazine or newspaper, or electronically transmitted on radio, television, or the Internet. Requests to the Publisher for permission should be made in writing and addressed to the Permissions Department using the address listed on the next page, check us out online, or email us at TravelMadeEasyGuide@gmail.com.

Published and distributed by Travel Made Easy (last update 12/06/2023).

The Essential Guide, The Kids Guide, Walking with Walt, Disney Made Easy, and Travel Made Easy are trademarks of Travel Made Easy, LLC.

This book is independent of the Walt Disney Company, Disney Enterprises, Inc. and any of its affiliates and sponsors.

Images, other Disney media, and any other Disney content copyrighted by The Walt Disney Company, Pixar, Star Wars, and any affiliates are used for promotional, information, and educational purposes. Reference to such materials is done so in compliance with the Fair Use Act of 1993.

Editor: Suzanne Albright

Contributing Authors: Jessie Sparks; Whitney Dakota Johnson, Owner and Author of Disneytipsandtrips.com; Terri Miller; Melissa Moore
Cover Design: Suzanne Albright
Cover & Interior Art: Gary Bilodeaux
Retail Price: $19.99

Limit of Liability/Disclaimer of Warranty

The information in this book is subject to change and should be verified when making travel plans.

Information is published in a variety of electronic formats. Some content that appears in print may differ from that found in electronic books.

ISBN: 978-1-956532-20-3

Manufactured in the United States of America

10 9 8 7 6 5 4 3 2 1

Disney Trivia

Across

3. The first name of Walt Disney's older brother and partner.
5. Mickey Mouse's lady friend.
6. In which state is Disneyland located?
8. April, May & ____ are the names of Daisy's nieces.
9. In what month was Walt Disney born?

Down

1. Who was Walt Disney's favorite president?
2. Walt considered this Missouri city to be his home town.
4. A lucky rabbit.
7. The first Disney theme park to open.
8. In what month did Disneyland open?

*Answers on Page 155

Table of Contents

Recent Changes: What to Expect . . 1
Meet Mr. Walter Elias Disney. . . . 6
A Dream is a Wish Your Heart Makes 11
    Important Dates in
    Disney History 14
Your Disneyland Trip! 15
    Here are a few things kids really
    love: 19
    Meeting Disney Characters. . 20
    What you need to know: . . . 21
    Minimum Height on Attractions 22
    Attraction Height Requirements
    24
Planning Your Trip is Fun! 25
Getting Ready for Disney Fun! . . . 29
Lightning Lanes & Genie+ 34
    Learn About Virtual Queues!. . 38
    Rider Switch (Child Swap) . . 38
Hidden Mickeys 41
Disneyland is Filled with Awesome
Fun! 45
Playing at the Parks! 51
    Final Hints for your Visit!. . . 54
    Things that Fright & Things that
    Excite! 56
Getting Around: Disneyland
Transportation 59
Let's Go to Disneyland Park. . . . 64
    Introduction to Disneyland . . 64
    Entertainment. 107
    Character Meet & Greets. . .110
Let's Go to
California Adventure! 113
    Highlights. 114
    8 Lands of
    California Adventure 115
    California Adventure Attractions 117
    Grizzly River Run. 127
    Entertainment. 129
    Character Meet & Greets. . .131

Other Fun Stuff at Disney
(and Other Nearby Places). 133
    Special Park Tours 134
    Downtown Disney 135
    Disney Cruise Line 136
    Fun Stuff Outside of Disney .137
Let's Eat at Disneyland! 141
    Kid Favorite Character Buffets 142
    Hotel Dining 147
Let's Stay at a Disney Hotel!. . . .149
    Disneyland Resorts (Hotels) .150
Puzzle Answers 154

Recent Changes: What to Expect

(updated December 06, 2023)

READ THIS SECTION WITH YOUR PARENTS. IT'S REALLY IMPORTANT!

Disney likes to change things up a lot. Sometimes those changes are affect how you and your family plan your trip.

Here is a *summary* (short description) of what you can expect.

Crowds at the Parks

Disneyland crowds are bigger than ever! They are heading to Disney in *droves* (huge numbers). This can make the parks feel very *congested* (meaning plugged up with people)!

Because there are so many people trying to do the same rides, see the same shows, and eat at the same restaurants, it's extra important that you get as many reservations as you can before your vacation.

Theme Park Operational Changes

Don't try to make last-minute plans. Disneyland Resort now requires an advanced reservation before entering either of the theme parks.

Your parents must buy tickets in *advance* (before your trip). Then they have to set up an account (either online or through the Disneyland app). Finally, they need to make a park reservation for every day of your trip.

You can still park hop if you have a ticket that lets you do so, but it's different than it used to be. You don't need a reservation for *both parks* on that day., but you can make one for both parks to make sure you get in to the second one. (If you don't, you might get turned away if the park is full!.) When you make the reservation, you have to pick which park is going to be the first one you visit that day.

Once you go to the first park, you have to wait until 11 am to change parks. If you get to Disneyland late and you don't make it to the first park you chose by 11 am, you can go to either park when you arrive.

FastPass and Disney MaxPass reservations have been replaced with the paid Lightning Lane reservation system. (This is super important — read the Lightning Lane chapter!)

This means, if you don't pay for Disney's Genie+ day-of reservation system (Tier 2 attractions) or pre-reserve a paid time for Tier 1 attractions, you must wait in a *stand-by queue* for each attraction.

Cast Members (Disney employees) are always working to improve *efficiencies* (reducing wasted time). The lines move much quicker than you might think (and often quicker than the posted wait times).

Disney Pass & Ticketing Options

You can't get some types of annual passes right now. This is because Disney wants to make sure visitors with regular tickets can get reservations.

Disney Transportation

If your parents drive to Disneyland or you're staying at a Disney hotel, there are Disney parking shuttles and a really neat monorail to take you to the parks.

Security Screenings

Standard security screenings are in place. If you have visited Disneyland before, you probably remember how that works. You walk through a metal detector, and a security guard might ask to check your backpacks, strollers, and other things for *prohibited* items (things you can't have in the parks).

Favorite Disney Treats

```
R R N C A S D H P N G N E E
R T R I E C Y L C R R G F L
U O N E A E C G P O E T R P
Y R I P T Y E F C Z Y U O P
N R I H I C A P R F S R Z A
G U M E B H O O R A T K E L
A H B G K P W N M R U E N E
D C E T T E O E I P F Y B M
P R E T Z E L S L F F L A A
F T C O R N D O G O D E N R
M I C K E Y B A R M D G A A
R O C T M M P N O U O R N C
Y R F B E I G N E T P E A I
O T S I R C E T N O M P P P
```

DOLE WHIP
POPCORN
GREY STUFF
FROZEN BANANA
MONTE CRISTO
TURKEY LEG
BEIGNET
CHURRO
MICKEY BAR
PRETZEL
CARAMEL APPLE
CORN DOG

Who were the Disney Brothers?

Walt and Roy Disney were close brothers since childhood. They even shared a bed together on their family farm in Marceline, Missouri, where they spent their early years. They moved to Chicago when they were still both quite young.

Walt was always the creative dreamer. As he grew up, he developed skills as an artist and started drawing cartoons.

Roy always watched over his younger brother. When they were young, Roy would push his younger brother around in a baby carriage, as they walked the streets together. When they grew up, Roy's protective nature became especially important, as he helped Walt pursue his dreams.

The brothers worked together from early on. In 1923, when Walt was only 21, the two co-founded the Disney Brothers Studio, and this relationship eventually evolved into the Walt Disney Company. Roy became a great businessman and ran the business. He worked easily with early investors and corporate partners. Roy once said, "My job is to help Walt do the things he wants to do."

Walt knew he couldn't succeed without his brother, who was his greatest supporter. To capture how important Roy's support of Walt was, there is a special bench in Town Square of Magic Kingdom with statues of Roy and Minnie Mouse sitting on it. These are the two unsung heroes in the world of Disney, playing important supporting roles to Walt and Mickey Mouse.

Meet Mr. Walter Elias Disney

Walt Disney was born on December 5, 1901, in Chicago, Illinois. That's over 100 years ago! He grew up on a farm where he was taught the importance of hard work and learning new things.

As a young kid, Walt was very imaginative and loved to daydream. He would look up and pretend the clouds in the sky above were animals, with the wind changing their shapes from one farmyard critter to another.

From an early age, he wished to become a cartoonist. In his wildest dreams, he probably couldn't have imagined that he would become as famous as he did!

In 1928, Walt created a little black and white mouse cartoon character. At first, Walt wanted to name this mouse "Mortimer." His wife,

Lillian Disney, didn't like that name and convinced Walt to name his mouse Mickey. That is how Mickey Mouse got his name!

Instant Animated Film Success. Mickey Mouse's first cartoon was *Plane Crazy*, a silent film. *Steamboat Willie* was the next cartoon Disney made. This second film is special because it was the first cartoon film to add *synchronized* sound that matched the action on the screen (called "synchronous sound"). This helped start a film revolution.

Walt's cartoons were very popular, and he *made a name for himself* (meaning he became well known).

Snow White and the Seven Dwarfs

Disney's big hit came in 1937 with the full-length movie (also called *feature film*) *Snow White and the Seven Dwarfs*. If you have not yet seen this animated movie, it is fun for everyone in the family!

Grimm Fairy Tales

Did you know *Snow White* is a tale from German folklore that dates all the way back to 1812? It was first written down by a couple of brothers, named Grimm. Disney was heavily influenced by their stories, which can also be seen in other movies.

Many people think Snow White is based on a real German royal named **Maria Sophia Margaretha Catharina, Baroness von und zu Erthal**, who was born in 1725!

"When I started Disneyland, my wife used to say, 'But why do you want to build an amusement park?' They're so dirty,' I told her that was just the point – mine wouldn't be."

~ Walt Disney

> *"The idea for Disneyland came about when my daughters were very young and Saturday was always Daddy's day with the two daughters. So we'd start out and try to go someplace, you know different things, and I'd take them to the merry-go-round and I took them different places and as I'd sit while they rode the merry-go-round and did all these things -- sit on a bench, you know, eating peanuts—I felt that there should be something built where the parents and the children could have fun together.*
>
> *So that's how Disneyland started. Well, it took many years...it was a period of maybe fifteen years developing. I started with many ideas, threw them away, started all over again. And eventually it evolved into what you see today at Disneyland. But it all started from a daddy with two daughters wondering where he could take them where he could have a little fun with them, too."*
>
> ~ **Walt Disney**

Walt became a world-famous movie producer. His first movies were cartoons. He also broke ground in "live-action" (which is a fancy way of saying they use real actors). Some of his productions included both **cartoons and live-action characters**, like Mary Poppins. Disney's skill at combining both types of films set the company apart in the industry.

Theme Park Developer. It was a full 30 years after his first film before Walt built his first theme park, Disneyland. As you may know, this is located in Anaheim, a city near Los Angeles, in southern California.

Where Did the Idea for a Theme Park Originate? Family was important to Walt. One Saturday, Walt took his wife and two daughters to an amusement park. His two young daughters loved the trip, but he felt the park was simply not clean or nice enough.

Walt didn't like that parents couldn't have fun on rides and doing other things with their children. He thought, "I wish there were a place where children and grown-ups could have fun together."

Mr. Disney and his brother became inspired and knew they could create a better and cleaner place for families. In fact, Walt made a rule that trash cans would be no more than 30 paces apart to make it easy and convenient for guests to throw away trash. Every person working at the park is required to pick up garbage they find as they walk about the park.

> **KID'S TRIVIA!**
>
> Chewing gum isn't sold anywhere on Disney property, because kids have a habit of spitting it out on the ground or sticking it under their seat!

There is a bronze statue of Walt with Mickey Mouse in front of the Sleeping Beauty's Castle at Disneyland. It's called the *Partners Statue*. The plaque on it talks about his dream:

I think most of all what I want Disneyland to be is a happy place...Where parents and children can have fun, together.

~ Walt Disney

Disney Characters

```
W A L L E D A I S Y D U C K
S D O N A L D D U C K Y R N
C U B A O T U L P A I E Y T
R O U I G O O F Y M K E B A
O D A G E N I E B A L O O C
O E S U O M Y E K C I M C E
G L B O L T I L G W O M C R
E T U M D Y T B A M B I O I
M M S D C D D H A N E M O H
C C D A U Y A O U R K A M S
D H U L I M Y L O M I W R E
U A I A A M B U E W P E O H
C B I P A E K O W O C E L C
K E S U O M E I N N I M R A
```

NEMO
GOOFY
CHIP
DAISY DUCK
BOLT
MICKEY MOUSE
PLUTO
BALOO
THUMPER
DONALD DUCK
MINNIE MOUSE
CHESHIRE CAT
SCROOGE MCDUCK
WALL-E
WOODY
DALE
DUMBO
BAMBI
MOWGLI
ARIEL
GENIE
ABU

Meet Mr. Walter Elias Disney

Adults are only kids grown up, anyway.

- Walt Disney

A Dream is a Wish Your Heart Makes

Important Dates in Disney History

JULY 17, 1955— DISNEYLAND OPENS IN ANAHEIM, CALIFORNIA

For years, Walt dreamed of the ideal place where grown-ups and kids could play together. It took him a long time to convince his brother, Roy, that they could make it work. It was going to cost a LOT of money, more money than the brothers could ever imagine—and more than the banks wanted to let them borrow. Walt and his brother had to risk everything they had worked for in order to build their theme park.

Fears of going broke haunted them, since they were striving for something bigger and better than anyone had tried before! However, at no point in time did the brothers give up on their dream!

Great success made Walt dream even bigger! After Disney's success with the Disneyland theme park and animated films, Walt dreamed of making his entertainment empire even greater. What he started would soon grow into a *fabulously huge* company.

He decided to open a new and much larger park somewhere where the weather was always warm, and close to where a lot of people in the United States lived. For this reason, he chose Orlando, Florida.

In 1955, Disneyland opens in Anaheim, California. Walt makes a dedication speech at the grand opening of the family park and says, "Here age relives fond memories of the past, and here youth may savor the challenge and promise of the future."

The park becomes a blockbuster success with millions of visitors from all over the world.

Kid's Trivia!

Disneyland was initially going to be called Mickey Mouse Park.

Walt Disney died December 15, 1966. While plans were made, work had not actually begun on the first Disney World theme park: Magic Kingdom. Roy believed in Walt's dreams and kept them alive. He honored his brother by naming the property the **Walt Disney World Resort**. Sadly, Roy died on December 20, 1971, just two-and-a-half months after the Magic Kingdom opened.

> **Did you know?** Over 20 million people travel to the Magic Kingdom each year—it's the most popular theme park in the world!

The Walt Disney Company Today

The Walt Disney Company is one of the world's largest companies in the entertainment and information business. It even owns several television channels, including ABC (American Broadcasting Company), ESPN, and Freeform. You probably watch these channels all the time and never realized they are owned by Disney.

The Walt Disney Company is known for its amazing movies and great TV shows. They create tons of products to go with those movies and shows, like books, toys, clothes and even apps for your phone. Disney is everywhere!

Disney History

Important Dates in Disney History

1901 December 5—Walt Disney is born in Chicago, Illinois

1928 First "synchronized sound" Mickey Mouse cartoon, *Steamboat Willie*

1937 First full-length animated film, *Snow White and the Seven Dwarfs*

1955 Disneyland park opens in Anaheim, California

1971 October 1—Magic Kingdom park opens in Florida

1980 Disneyland's 25th anniversary

1982 October 1—Epcot park opens in Florida

1983 Tokyo Disneyland opens (In Japan's capital city)

1989 May 1—Disney-MGM Studios opens (now Disney's Hollywood Studios)

1992 Disneyland Paris opens (in France's capital city)

1998 April 22—Animal Kingdom park opens in Florida

2001 February 8—California Adventure opens in California

2005 Disneyland's 50th Anniversary

2012 Disney purchases the Lucasfilm company (Star Wars) for $4 billion

2016 Star Wars expansion begins

2019 Star Wars: Galaxy's Edge land opens in Disneyland

2021 Walt Disney World's 50th anniversary

2023 The Disney Company's 100th anniversary

Your Disneyland Trip!

Kid's Tip!

Take notes as you read through this book to help remember important things. Write down the name of each attraction and show you want to see.

HINT: When you see the *Kid's Tip!* icon, it means one of our readers shared important information with us.

Color the Train!

If you are reading this book, it probably means one thing...You are planning a very special trip...

You're going to Disneyland!

Disneyland is "the Happiest Place on Earth" and the absolute best place for kids! It is also great for families because it lets out the hidden child within every adult - everyone can play and have a blast!

Disneyland is WAY MORE than just an amusement park. Most kids have been to a state or county fair and think that Disneyland is about the same size and has the same number of fun things to see and do. A county or state fair is not even close! Take any one you have ever been to and multiply the fun and excitement by 100!

This book tells you about everything you need to know to become an expert on all things Disney. It's filled with awesome advice from kids just like you!

Anaheim is a large city in Southern California where you can soak up the sun pretty much all year round.

Disneyland is located in the heart of Anaheim.

From Interstate 5 (I-5), look for the Disneyland exits. Just tell your folks to follow the signs!

Use the directions in this book to help your parents get there.

If your parents are driving south (from LAX Airport or Sacramento), take Interstate 5 (I-5) southbound. When you see the Disneyland Drive exit, tell your parents to take it. Have them drive in one of the two right lanes and follow the signs to Disneyland parking. It's that easy!

> **Did you know?** Walt Disney World in Florida is known as "The Most Magical Place on Earth."

Disneyland has a ton of stuff to do.

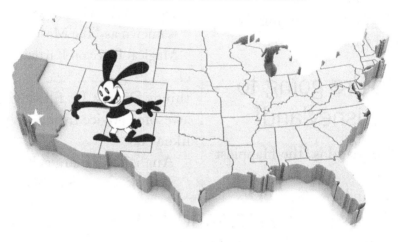

Oswald the Lucky Rabbit was created by Walt Disney and Ub Iwerks in 1927 for Universal Pictures.

If your parents are driving north on Interstate 5 (from John Wayne Airport or San Diego), have them take the Disney Way exit and follow the signs to Disneyland parking.

If you're parents are driving north and going to a Disney hotel first, have your parents take the Harbor Boulevard exit. When they reach the first light at Ball Road, tell them to turn left. Have them take another left when you reach Disneyland Drive and follow the signs.

The "Theme Park" signs take you right to the Disneyland parking. Tell your parents to drive in the two right lanes for the hotel parking and Downtown Disney.

Remember to look for the signs. Don't miss it!

Did you know? The very first theme park was not Disneyland. It was the nearby Knott's Berry Farm, which got its start from a popular chicken restaurant!

You are going to have so much fun experiencing amazing amusement rides and seeing live stage shows. You can also meet many Disney Characters, like Mickey Mouse himself!

Surprises!

Surprises come in all forms, from things that make you laugh to those that might scare you ever so slightly. Some kids don't like loud and dark rides. Other kids don't like thrill rides where you go super-fast and take unexpected turns or drops. (If your mom or dad's back is bad, they must be careful on fast rides, too!)

Noises. If you don't like loud noises, ask your parents to bring ear plugs or other hearing protection. (It will also help you nap during the day if your hotel room is noisy!)

Darkness. Some kids are afraid of the dark. Remember, no scary monsters can get you at Disney! In fact, there's usually a ton of fun waiting inside the dark rides. You may be surprised to find out you're laughing by the time you leave!

> ### Kid's Tip!
> Bring an eye mask to keep the light out of your eyes when you sleep.

Water. There are also a couple of rides that can get you wet. Remember to take a change of clothes with you, or those water rides will leave you soggy all day!

Look for These *Attraction Reactions*™!

 Thrills & Excitement!

 You May Get **Soaked!**

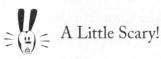
A Little Scary!

 Dizzy/Motion Sickness Possible!

Everyone here wants to help you have a fantastic vacation filled with happy family memories! Read along and let us help you plan a perfect trip.

We know this is a big book. You don't have to read it all. Skim it now really fast to find what you like the most. Pick it up again later to read those

> ### Kid's Tip!
>
> Take this book on your trip with you. Remember to pack it in your luggage! You can glance back through it when you visit each park so you don't miss a thing. It also gives you something to look at while you wait in lines.

sections all the way through and study the most helpful parts.

Keep Lists. We have lists at the end of each theme park section to help you decide what to do each day. With your list, you can keep track of everything you don't want to miss.

Even if a wild ride looks scary—don't worry! You're completely safe. Disney adds a lot of fun special effects and makes sure there's no real danger. Just remember it's all make-believe. Just like all the action and scary stuff you see on television and at the movies, nothing here is real – except for the fun! Think of it like a big movie set.

Here are a few things kids really love:

- *Peter Pan's Flight* and *Splash Mountain* at Magic Kingdom; and
- *Monsters, Inc. Mike and Sully to the Rescue* and *Mater's Junkyard Jamboree* at California Adventure.

> ### Kid's Tip!
>
> Even though the Matterhorn and Space Mountain seem scary, most kids really love them. They also get a thrill plunging down Splash Mountain and Grizzly River Run!

> ### Kid's Tip!
>
> Don't forget to smile on the rides. Disney takes photos of you on a lot of them! On the rides that take automatic pictures, there is a preview area where you can see your photo right after you hop off the ride. Make sure to stop by and see how you looked. They can be really funny sometimes!

Meeting Disney Characters

Character Meet and Greets, Photographs and Autographs. Take time to meet all your favorite characters and get their autographs! Bring your autograph book and a big pen, because the characters have big hands. (Some of them have a hard time holding skinny pens.)

If you have a camera, be sure to take it! Otherwise, ask your parents to snap the shots that YOU are going to want to share with your friends when you get home. Your parents can also buy pictures from Disney's PhotoPass system. These are photos taken by professional Disney photographers and automated camera systems in all the best spots, including the coolest rides!

Let's Learn about Characters!

A character is a real-life version of the animated creatures and people in Disney movies and television shows. Although these characters may appear very small in film, they are actually as big as grown-ups!

There are two different kinds of characters: known as **Face** and **Fur**.

Face Characters. These look a lot like regular people and include Princesses, Princes, Peter Pan, Mary Poppins, and even Alice in Wonderland, to name a few. They are called face characters because you can see their faces and talk to them.

Fur Characters. Fur characters are mostly animals. These include some of your favorite characters, such as the "**Fab 5**" (*fab* is short for fabulous): Mickey, Minnie, Goofy, Donald and Pluto. Fur characters love big hugs, but they do not talk. Instead, they use gestures to communicate – kind of like sign language, but easy for everyone to understand!

Character Meet & Greet Schedules. Character Meet

Let your inner daredevil come out to play!

and Greets are at scheduled times and places. They take a picture with you and sign autographs if you bring something to write on.

Find Character Greeting times in the <u>Times Guide</u> at each park's Guest Relations or at the Guest Information Desk (concierge desk) if you're staying at a Disney hotel. If you have additional questions, ask your hotel Cast Member to check the <u>Character Hotline</u> (only available at a Disney hotel) to see when and where a character is available.

What you need to know:

TRIP LENGTH: Seeing all the important stuff at Disneyland takes at least two or three full days inside the parks, and that's not counting all the other stuff to do in California.

Even if you can only visit the California sun for a few days, it is still better than no fun at all. Some families can plan a once-in-a-lifetime trip that lasts two full weeks, while others stay only four or five days at a time.

There is no perfect length for a Disneyland vacation; what is right for some is not right for others. If your family can afford a longer stay and want to visit some of the other California attractions, try to plan at least five to seven days – especially if it is your first trip!

Disneyland is so big that you need more than a single day to see and do everything. But even if you can only come for a day or two, you can immediately start planning your next trip to catch everything you missed!

Did you know? Trips to Disneyland Resort should take at least five days. This has been voted the best length of stay for a family vacation!

There are tons of really cool things to do and see at Disneyland. No matter how long your stay is, you might not see it all, and that's not even counting all the other stuff in California.

As you go through this book, think about what you really want to make sure you see or do. Talk to your family, too. Everyone will have their own ideas. Work together to come up with a good plan to make everyone happy.

> **HINT FOR CHAMPIONS!**

<u>The early bird really does get the worm at Disney.</u> This is no time to be lazy. Get up early! Aim to arrive at the parks *before* opening! Sleep in and you may miss out on the best rides. Plan on being the one that gets the rest of your family to rise out of bed in the mornings!

It's not advertised, but Disneyland Park lets you enter Main Street (the shopping area) 30 minutes before its official opening time. The rides aren't actually running yet, but this lets you get to your first adventure quickly!

Opening Time. Parks usually open at 8:00 a.m. or 9:00 a.m.

Closing Time. Parks usually stay open until 9:00 p.m. or 10:00 p.m., but they might stay open past midnight on really busy days!

Check Operating Hours. Ask a parent to check the hours ("operating hours") for each theme park on the day your family is planning to visit. Remind them that this information is on the Disneyland app, or they can ask at the Guest Information desk at the hotel.

Plan where you're going to eat before you go!! Tell your parents they can save a lot of time by making lunch and dinner reservations for popular restaurants before you go on your trip. They can reserve dining times as early as two months (60 days) before your trip. You can even meet some of your favorite Disney friends, like Mickey and Minnie, when you eat at some of the really nice places. This means you won't have to wait in line to see them at the parks!

Minimum Height on Attractions

Do you know how tall you are? We know you're really excited about all the rides. Some rides are made just for big kids, though.

That means you have to be tall enough for some

attractions. In other words, there is a minimum height required for some bigger rides.

Get your measuring tape out and ask a parent to help you figure out your height. You can compare it with the following list to see if you are tall enough for the big kid stuff.

We know it can be disappointing if you're a little too short to go on that really awesome attraction. Just remember, it's to keep you safe. You wouldn't want to slip out of a harness and fall! Plus, you can use it as a reason to go to Disneyland (or Walt Disney World!) when you're a couple of years older!

Here are rides with minimum height requirements for each theme park:

Disneyland
- Autopia: 32in (82cm) to ride; 54in (137cm) to drive
- Big Thunder Mountain Railroad: 40in (102cm)
- Chip n' Dale's GADGETcoaster: 35in (89cm)
- Indiana Jones Adventure: 46in (117cm)
- Matterhorn Bobsleds: 42in (107cm)
- Millenium Falcon: Smugglers Run: 38in (102cm)
- Space Mountain: 40in (102cm)
- Splash Mountain: 40in (102cm)
- Star Tours: 40in (102cm)
- Star Wars: Rise of the Resistance: 40in (102cm)

California Adventure
- Goofy's Sky School: 42in (107cm)
- Grizzly River Run: 42in (107cm)
- GOTG - Mission: BREAKOUT!: 40in (102cm)
- Incredicoaster: 48in (122cm)
- Jumpin' Jellyfish: 40in (102cm)
- Radiator Springs Racers: 40in (102cm)
- Redwood Creek Challenge Trail (Rock Wall & Zip Line Only): 42in (107cm)
- Silly Symphony Swings: 40in (102cm) tandem; 48in (122cm) single
- Soarin' Around the World: 40in (102cm)

Attraction Height Requirements

Minimum Height	Disneyland	California Adventure
54"	Autopia Note: Must be 32" to ride with an older driver.	
48"		Incredicoaster Silly Symphony Swings (Single)
46"	Indiana Jones Adventure	
42"	Matterhorn Bobsleds	Goofy's Sky School Grizzly River Run Redwood Creek Challenge Trail (Rock Wall & Zip Line)
40"	Big Thunder Mountain Railroad Space Mountain Splash Mountain Star Tours Star Wars: Rise of the Resistance	GOTG - Mission: BREAKOUT! Jumpin' Jellyfish Radiator Springs Racers Silly Symphony Swings (Tandem) Soarin' Around the World
38"	Millennium Falcon: Smugglers Run	
35"	Chip n' Dale's GADGETcoaster	
32"	Autopia Note: Must be 54" to ride alone.	

Your Disneyland Trip!

Planning Your Trip is Fun!

We know you like reading. How? Because this book is in your hands!

Maybe you're someone who loves writing and drawing pictures about Disneyland. (We'd love to see your art and read your stories, too! Feel free to send them to us after getting your parent's permission. You may see them in a future edition!)

A lot of our readers love playing sports, using a computer, singing, dancing and making music, too. Most of us like watching live shows where we can sing along to our favorite songs.

Did you know that you can do all of these things at Disneyland?

Are you someone who likes taking photographs and shooting videos? There are a lot of picture opportunities to uncover while you explore.

Photo Spots. Disney PhotoPass photographers are at some of the coolest locations in the parks, but there are lots of other great spots to take photos. Look for "Photo Spot" signs to find great places to get a memorable snapshot.

Treats! Of course, you're going to love all the tasty treats that Disney offers, including churros, Mickey Mouse ice cream bars, popcorn, and the famous soft, frozen pineapple ice cream treat called a *Dole Whip*. It's yummy!

Meals. Look for the section in this book that shares lots of food choices kids love!

Favorite Rides Lists. At the end of each park section, we have a table that lists all the must-see rides and attractions. Of course, pretty much everything at Disney is a kid-pleaser! Our list just lets you know which rides you should put first on your list, so there is no chance you are going to miss them. Make sure you look over these tables!

Attraction Refurbishments. Disney sometimes shuts down rides to make repairs. If a ride is important to you, ask an adult to check for it on the list of scheduled maintenance at the following website:

https://www.disneytouristblog.com/disneyland-refurbishment-calendar/.

Meeting the Characters. You can spend days just meeting your favorite Disney stars, but don't get so caught up that you miss out on the rides and shows. Pick only two or three characters to meet at each park to give plenty of time for other fun stuff.

Live Performances. Singing. Dancing. Action. You get everything at the stage shows in Disneyland Park and California Adventure. Don't forget to see shows like *Disney Junior Dance Party!* and *Fantasmic!* (We'll tell you more about these later.)

Hotels

Kids especially like the pools at Disney hotels. Some of them have awesome themes and waterslides. Read more about these cool experiences and more in our section about resort hotels towards the end of this book.

Getting Ready for Disney Fun!

Ask a parent to help you figure out what the weather in California should be like when you visit. Pay special attention to the season in which you're traveling to Disneyland.

California is usually extra warm and dry, but it can get very chilly any time in the late fall through early spring (especially November to February). Even if the day is warm, it can cool down at night. Don't forget to take along a warm jacket and sweater if you visit in these months, *just in case*.

Packing Your Luggage. Leave packing to your

> **Kid's Tip!**
>
> Bring an umbrella or poncho if the weather report gives a 40% or greater chance of rain. You can keep enjoying the parks, while everyone else runs for cover!
>
> A poncho is very easy to fold up and put away when the rain clears up. It will also help keep you dry on the water rides! (Tell your parents to buy ponchos at a dollar store before your vacation starts—the ponchos in the parks are pretty pricey!)

> **Summer Heat Warning.** It gets really hot at least half the year in California. Pay attention when you are playing in the sun. It is important to note if you stop sweating. This is a serious sign that you are overheated. Keep an eye on your parents and siblings to watch for these warnings, too.
>
> • Keep drinking water <u>even when you don't feel thirsty</u>. Take a break every 20 minutes for a long sip on hot summer days.
> • There is an increased risk if you run around a lot.
> • If you start to feel faint, lightheaded or dizzy, tell an adult!

parents. Just double check that they bring:

- Sunscreen and bug spray – a painful sunburn ruins your vacation, and no one likes to scratch bug bites.
- Shorts and pants. Opt for shorts unless you are visiting from October through February.
- Long and short-sleeved shirts, sweaters and jackets.
- Lightweight clothing and comfortable shoes that you can spend a lot of time walking in. They should be well-worn in. Do not bring brand new shoes, no matter how cute or cool they are. It's easy for feet to get blisters, and these are no fun.
- Bathing suit.
- Hat and sunglasses.
- A favorite Disney costume, such as a princess or pirate costume, to dress as a favorite character at the park!

Clothing. Wear layers if it might get cool, like sweaters and jackets over your T-shirt. When you wear layers, it means that as you warm up, you can take off one piece of outer clothing. Since you keep them with you in a backpack, when it starts to cool down in the evening, you can put the layers back on to warm up.

Kid's Tip!

Leave room in your suitcase for souvenirs to take home with you!

Kid's Tip!

Ask your parents nicely for a brand new Disney T-Shirt as soon as you get to the park. Better yet, have them buy you one before you go. It'll cost less money and be a fun thing to wear as you travel to Disney!

Fun In the Sun Warning!

Remember to Use Sunscreen and Wear Sunglasses!

Sunscreen. Make sure to use lots of sunscreen and reapply throughout the day! This is especially important for people from the northern states and those with fair skin, but anyone can get burned if they are not careful.

> **Did you know?** As much as 80% of the sun's rays get through the clouds on a hazy day. You need protection if you are spending any time outside, not just when you go to the beach. Ultraviolet (UV) rays from the sun can burn the skin, leaving you in pain and misery during your trip. If your parent asks, tell them to get a Sun Protection Factor (SPF) of at least 30, including what is called "Broad Spectrum."

Please remember that it only takes <u>15 to 30 minutes</u> for your skin to burn if it is not protected by clothing or sunscreen. Because the lotion does not last all day, you will need to put more on every couple of hours, and even more often if you are playing in a pool.

It is important to wear sunglasses to protect your eyes. If you play in the water, glare from the sun is even more dangerous to our young eyes.

Kid's Tip!

Don't Forget! Ask your parents for dark sunglasses and a hat with a wide brim. The California sun is super bright!

Plan & Pack Like A Pro!

Tell your parents to download and use our free planning and packing tools at:

bit.ly/DisneyPlanners

There's a Packing Checklist, Budget Worksheet, Attraction Planner, and Dining Planner - and they don't cost a penny!

Lightning Lanes & Genie+

Did you know you can reserve a time to go on some of your favorite attractions? Disney has a reservation system that lets you walk to the front of the line for most attractions.

With a reservation, you get on a ride almost as quick as lightning. That's why Disney named the special *queues* for people with reservations *Lightning Lanes*!

Lightning Lane reservations cost money. Check with your parents to see if they want to pay extra money to save time or use that money for other things.

If your parents don't get Lightning Lane reservations scheduled for popular rides, you have to go through the regular line (called the *standby queue* – pronounced just like the letter "Q"). This can take a lot more time, so be prepared.

The best option is to get your family to the park really early in the morning. Otherwise, just keep an eye on the line throughout the day to see when wait times are low!

The reservation system is confusing. Most adults don't understand it, so your parents may need your help!

There are two different reservation systems: *Genie+* or *Individual Lightning Lane* reservations. How you make and pay for a reservation depends on how popular the ride is.

Look at it this way. Some attractions are so popular, people wait for hours to go on them. We call those Tier 1 attractions. Brand new rides and shows are often Tier 1.

Other rides are still fun, but the wait time for them is usually under one hour. We call those Tier 2 attractions. A lot of *oldie-but-goody* rides are Tier 2, including *Peter Pan's Flight* and *Soarin' Around the World*.

There are also Tier 3 attractions. These are the ones you can usually walk right on with almost no wait. *Casey Jr. Circus Train* and *Sleeping Beauty Castle Walkthrough* are good examples of Tier 3.

Tier 3 attractions don't have Lightning Lanes available. You can't reserve a time to visit them, because you don't need to!

Tier 2 attractions are part of the Genie+ reservation system. You can pay $30 or more per person for the Genie+ (*Genie Plus*) service each day of your vacation. If

> The best Lightning Lane reservations run out fast, so you have to hurry!

Kid's Tip!

Use the Disneyland app to see when the wait times to get on a ride are low. The app is great for ordering food, reserving Lightning Lanes, checking out showtimes and lots of other things. For really popular rides, you might have to wait for a parade or the fireworks to see wait times go down.

there are four people in your family, Genie+ costs at least $120 per day.

That can really add up if you use Genie+ every day! Fortunately, you can choose to use it (or not) for as many days as you want.

Your parents may only want to pay for Genie+ if the park is super busy, like Disneyland Park usually is.

There are usually two Tier 1 attractions at each park. You can't reserve Tier 1 attractions through Genie+. To get on a Tier 1 ride quickly, you need an Individual Lightning Lane reservation.

Individual means you need to pay for a separate reservation for each popular ride you want to do. In other words, if you want to go on *Star Wars: Rise of the Resistance*, each person must pay money for just that single ride.

Some Tier 1 attractions are more popular than others. Also, a park might be busier on one day and slower on another. Because of this, there may be more or less people trying to go on a Tier 1 ride.

Disney changes the amount they charge for Individual Lightning Lane reservations each day. If it's a really busy day and a really popular ride, you pay more. If you go to Disney during a slow season (meaning less people are traveling), you pay less.

Each Individual Lightning Lane reservation costs anywhere from $15 to $25 per person. That's a lot of money.

Kid's Tip!

Disney also changes it them park ticket prices based on the same system. That means a trip to Disney costs less when fewer people are able to go, like when you're in school. It costs more when lots of people want to go, like during summer break!

Make sure your parents know to include it in the trip *budget*. (The budget is how much money your family has available to spend on the vacation.)

Using Disney's Genie

Most people just call it "Genie." However, you may

sometimes hear it called "Genie *Plus*." They mean almost the same thing.

Genie is the free portion of the service. Genie+ is the part you have to pay to use.

With Genie, you can make an *itinerary* for each day of your trip. The itinerary is a list of things you want to do each day.

Genie makes it super easy. Genie is part of the Disneyland app, so make sure your parents download it! (You can probably help your parent(s) set up the app!)

Use Genie to choose the calendar day and the park you're visiting. After that, simply answer a few questions about your likes and dislikes.

Genie will automatically create a suggested itinerary. You can select an item on the itinerary to change it if you don't like something.

Once you have the itinerary, Genie makes suggestions for Genie+ and Individual Lightning Lane Reservations. Your parents can simply click a button on the app to start reserving rides!

Tell your parents they have to wait until the morning of each park visit to make reservations for Genie+ or Individual Lightning Lane attractions. (They can pay for Genie+ in advance, but they can't start making reservations until the day you visit!)

They can make the first Tier 2 reservation as early as 7:00 a.m. the morning of your visit. You can't do it before that time!

Each time you use a Genie+ reservation, you can make a new reservation through the app.

You can only have one Genie+ reservation at a time. Also, you can't reserve the same attraction more than once per day.

It's a little different for Tier 1 attractions.

You can only buy two Individual Lightning Lane Reservations per day. This means you have to choose which two of the most popular you want to do for every day of your trip.

Just like with Genie+, you must wait until the day of your visit to make a Tier 1 reservation.

If you're staying at a Disney hotel, you can reserve your

Learn About Virtual Queues!

Disney sometimes uses virtual queues for brand new rides, like *Mickey & Minnie's Runaway Railway*. Rather than stand in a line, you sign up to enter the queue *virtually* through the Disneyland App.

Virtual queues open at 7:00 a.m. each morning and fill up right away. If you don't get a spot in a virtual queue, there is no standby queue.

The only other way you can go on that attraction is to pay for an Individual Lightning Lane reservation!

Rider Switch (Child Swap)

If you have a younger brother or sister who is too scared or too small to go on any ride, you are in luck! Disney has a way to make sure all of the adults get a turn to go on the ride, and it means the older kids get to go on it twice!!!

What is Rider Switch? You and your folks simply meet the queue attendant and ask to do the "Rider Switch." The Cast Member counts the number of kids in the party and gives the adults in the group a paper pass. This allows one or more parent (or other adults) to take the older kids on the ride, while the other waits with the younger kid(s). Then, when you're done riding the first time, the waiting adult can use the pass to take all the bigger kids on the ride a second time!

Tier 1 Lightning Lane times as early as 7:00 a.m.

If you're staying off-property (at a non-Disney hotel), you have to wait until the park opens for the day to make a Tier 1 Lightning Lane reservation.

Because Tier 1 rides are so popular, that means all the reservations might be sold out by the time the park opens!

If some Tier 1 rides are really important for your family, make sure your parents know. They may decide to stay at a Disney hotel to make sure you get all the Lightning Lane reservations you want!

The scheduled time lets you show up to the ride or attraction any time over an hour-long period of time, or "window." For example, if your Lightning Lane reservation is 1:05 p.m. to 2:05 p.m., you can arrive anytime in that window.

- **Hint:** There is a "grace period" for most Lightning Lane reservation windows; you can show up 5 minutes early or arrive 15 minutes late and may still be admitted to the attraction.

After reading this book, think about which rides and attractions you absolutely HAVE to see. Then, ask your mom or dad to reserve Lighting Lanes times for them.

Kid's Tip!

If a stay in a Disney hotel doesn't fit the trip budget, tell your parents they can book just one or two nights of your vacation in one of them.

You can still get all the perks for those days, including early booking of Lightning Lane reservations!

LET US HELP! Here is a list of the rides and attractions you may want to consider. They are the Must-See rides for which we think you really need Lightning Lane reservations. A star next to the name means it's a really popular attraction. Two stars means it's one of the most popular rides and very high in demand!

Disneyland Park

- Autopia
- ★ Peter Pan's Flight
- ★★ Big Thunder Mountain Railroad
- Buzz Lightyear's Astro Blasters
- Haunted Mansion
- ★★ Indiana Jones™ Adventure
- "it's a small world"
- ★★ Matterhorn Bobleds
- ★★ Mickey & Minnie's Runaway Railway
- Millennium Falcon: Smugglers Run
- ★ Roger Rabbit's Car Toon Spin
- ★ Splash Mountain
- ★★ Space Mountain
- Star Tours - The Adventures Continue
- ★★ Star Wars: Rise of the Resistance

Disneyland has 15 attractions we rate **Must-See** (see the end of the Disneyland section). They all have Lightning Lanes available.

Just remember, there are tons of rides at Disneyland Park. Because there are so many things to do at this park, it is impossible to see them all unless you are visiting the park for two or more days.

California Adventure

- ★ Grizzly River Run
- ★★ Guardians of the Galaxy — Mission: BREAKOUT!
- ★ Incredicoaster
- Monsters, Inc. Mike & Sully to the Rescue!
- ★★ Radiator Springs Racers
- ★★ Soarin' Around the World
- ★ Toy Story Midway Mania!

California Adventure has 10 attractions we rate **Must-See** (see the end of the California Adventure section). Most of them have Lightning Lanes available.

The attractions on the two lists above are favorites among kids.

Hidden Mickeys

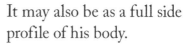

Disney "Imagineers" are the people behind the scenes who design all the fun. The job title combines the words "imagination" with "engineering."

What are Hidden Mickeys?

Description

Search for the classic 3-circle Mickey silhouette.

The so-called "classic design" uses three circles to represent Mickey's face and large, round ears. This is the most basic and standard kind of Hidden Mickey, but there are other kinds. A Hidden Mickey could also be:

- a detailed image of his ears and face (or body).
- a 3-D representation.
- a profile: Mickey may appear as a side profile (often showing only 3/4 of his face, head and ears). It may also be as a full side profile of his body.
- a full-length silhouette of him from the front.

Sometimes Hidden Mickeys include just his handprints, gloves, shoes, or ears. Even finding his initials or name in unexpected locations could be a Hidden Mickey. (Though very rare, other Disney characters are also "hidden," including Minnie Mouse, Donald Duck, Goofy and others.)

Discover Hidden Mickeys in the shadows or lights, in gemstones, rocks and trees. Look up to the sky murals painted on ceilings and perhaps see a Hidden Mickey cloud. At night, you might find one in the fireworks as they explode in the sky. They can be found in any type of drawings or decoration, as well as walls, murals and wood carvings.

> Imagineers have hidden lots of Mickey ears and silhouettes in unexpected places throughout Disneyland just for you to find! It's like a fun treasure hunt to try to find them all.

Hidden Mickeys are meant to be discrete or secret. When you notice one, it will be in a random place that surprises you. They have been "hidden" intentionally and integrated into design elements in a way that would not otherwise be expected.

What Hidden Mickeys are NOT. While often found in plain sight, a Hidden Mickey is <u>not</u> a regular Mickey drawing, like something printed on a sign or restaurant's menu. You can't claim anything used in promotional advertising.

- A Hidden Mickey is also <u>not</u> the shape you see in a sign or shop window display where the symbol would be expected.
- It is <u>not</u> decorative placements in windows, walls or gates.
- Likewise, it is <u>not</u> the obvious markings on manhole covers or other such construction designs.

Hidden Mickey Etiquette

Proper etiquette means that you should always be considerate of Cast Members and other guests. If you are searching in a line, move out of the way and let other guests pass you. Having manners requires that you don't interrupt another guest in line, at a restaurant or anywhere else without asking permission first.

If you let those around you know what you are doing, they may join in to help you look. They may have never heard about Hidden Mickeys!

Here are a few Hidden Mickey locations to get you started:

Big Thunder Ranch. Look for the pile of horseshoes near Big Thunder Mountain Railroad.

Gadget's Go Coaster. Look at the stones in the wall while waiting in the queue for some stones that create a familiar shape.

Disneyland Hotel. Look at the lobby carpet for a rare side silhouette.

Animation Academy. Look around at the shelves on the room.

Mater's Junkyard Jamboree. Look up at the hubcaps on the ceiling of the queue.

Soarin' Around the World. Take a close look at the hot air balloon scene when it comes on the screen. The balloons create the classic shape!

Mickey and Friends Parking Lot. Head to Section 2A of the parking structure for a special design put into the concrete floor.

Disney Villains

A	M	A	L	E	F	I	C	E	N	T	Y	R	T
L	I	H	R	A	T	I	G	A	N	Z	R	N	O
U	A	E	F	R	O	L	L	O	A	S	G	E	R
S	E	R	G	A	R	C	A	O	H	A	I	Y	A
R	N	O	K	O	A	E	D	O	R	A	Z	N	F
U	R	R	K	I	B	A	I	R	B	M	N	R	A
S	E	D	A	H	N	A	K	L	A	A	N	S	J
Y	I	D	H	A	K	G	N	A	I	G	A	R	C
T	C	K	O	Y	A	O	C	R	A	C	U	F	L
F	Z	A	S	C	A	R	S	A	E	D	A	T	A
G	G	A	S	T	O	N	Y	Y	N	H	N	F	Y
E	F	U	Y	N	A	H	S	H	K	D	C	G	T
N	H	A	K	E	R	E	H	S	F	E	Y	L	O
C	S	Y	N	D	R	O	M	E	E	R	S	S	N

SYNDROME
FROLLO
SHERE KAHN
JAFAR
FACILIER
GASTON
SHAN YU
HANS
KAA
HADES
MALEFICENT
RATIGAN
CHERNABOG
SCAR
KING CANDY
CLAYTON
SYKES
YZMA
URSULA

Disneyland is Filled with Awesome Fun!

Color Disneyland's Entrance!

Disneyland Resort has two theme parks and a shopping district. The parks are Disneyland Park and Disney's California Adventure.

It isn't very big compared to other Disney Resorts (such as Walt Disney World), but it's full of things to do and see.

In fact, Disneyland Park has the most attractions of any Disney theme park!

Because it's packed with so many attractions, Disneyland Resort seems much larger than its total of 500 acres. You will go "Wow!" when you see it all!

Summary

Disneyland Park (1955)

Sleeping Beauty's Castle sits in the hub (center) of the park with six lands surrounding it.

Main Street, U.S.A. is the first land you see. The other lands you encounter are Adventureland, Critter Country, Galaxy's Edge, New Orleans Square, Frontierland, Toontown, Fantasyland and Tomorrowland.

KID'S TRIVIA!

Disney purchased the *Star Wars* franchise in 2012. They built an entire Star Wars land called Galaxy's Edge in Disneyland Park that opened in 2019. It's out of this world!

Millennium Falcon: Smugglers Run. Become an international space smuggler as you pilot the galaxy's fastest space ship!

Star Wars: Rise of the Resistance. Take on the First Order in an epic battle with the Resistance.

KID'S TRIVIA!

Disneyland is sometimes referred to as the Magic Kingdom. Even though Disneyland looks a lot like the Magic Kingdom in Florida, there are quite a few differences. For instance, Disneyland has two more lands: New Orleans Square and Critter Country!

Disneyland is Filled with Awesome Fun!

Disney's California Adventure (1989)

This park celebrates all things California, from mountains to the sea. It also highlights California's influence on show business and the magic of movie-making!

Guardians of the Galaxy—Mission: BREAKOUT! This is the definitely the most out-of-this-world *drop ride* around. Disney set the standard for this type of fun, and you will not be disappointed!

Incredicoaster. This is one of the most exciting roller coasters at Disneyland. It has loop-de-loops and turns galore!

Toy Story Midway Mania. This 4-D shooting game stars your favorite Toy Story characters. The whole family will love riding through a midway-like area and blasting up things to score points.

Resort Pools

Lots of Anaheim hotels have great pools. Some even rival the water parks with fun stuff to do!

If you're staying at a Disney hotel, you know their top-notch resort pools are great. The Disney resorts also have water slides at their pools!

Planning is half the fun! Help your parents start planning early. It usually takes at least **three** months to take care of all the details! Here are some things you can help decide:

- How many days do you need at each park?
- Are there other California theme parks you want to visit?
- When is the best time of year to go?
- What clothing should you pack?
  - » Remember: if you go to an area water park, your parents are going to have to pack extra clothing to keep dry ones with you!
- Which characters can you meet and where can you find them?
- Which attractions do you want to experience?
- Are there special restaurants you want to try?

WRITE IT DOWN! Get out note paper and a pencil to take notes! Make a plan!

There are more than 100 attractions at Disneyland! This means that you need to create a schedule, so you don't miss what matters to you.

Keep adding notes and then write out your master list when you are ready to leave home. Start with two sheets of paper, one page for each park. Write the name of one park at the top of each page. When you read about something that you want to do, write it down on the appropriate piece of paper.

Kid's Tip!

Use *Post-it* notes, if you can. They let you move things around without having to rewrite your notes.

Disneyland is Filled with Awesome Fun!

Oswald the Lucky Rabbit was created by Walt Disney and Ub Iwerks in 1927 for Universal Pictures.

When you are finished, pick your top five "must see" attractions and then number the rest of the attractions in order of importance.

Afterwards, review your notes, print a schedule and rewrite your choices on it.

Share this final list with the other kids who are traveling with you to make sure you can agree on what to do. Then, share your plans with your parents (or whichever adult is taking care of things). They need it so that they can complete their vacation planning (like getting reservations to your favorite restaurants!) and scheduling your Lightning Lane reservations.

After all the reservations have been made, print your final schedule (called an itinerary). Give a copy to everyone who is traveling with you.

Children never get lost at Disney! Disney is the only place that understands that it is not kids that get lost, but our parents!

If you ever get separated from your family (It's easy to do with all the things to see and do!), find any Disney employee. (Disney employees are called Cast Members – look for a Disney name tag to tell if it's a Cast Member.)

Tell them your family is lost and needs help finding you. They put all their efforts into finding your folks quickly, so you can get on with your fun.

To make sure everyone is easy to find, have your parents take a picture of you and your brothers and sisters each morning. If they find a Cast Member, they can show them what you look like and what you're wearing - this can help speed up the process of reuniting everyone!

Kid's Tip!

Ask your parent to take a picture of your itinerary with their smart phone in case anyone loses their printed copy!

Disney Trivia!

Did you know that Walt Disney didn't like people pointing with their index fingers? He thought this action looked rude. This is why Cast Members are taught to use a "**Disney point**" with both the index finger and middle finger, together. They can also indicate direction with their entire hand opened. This gesture is called an "open-palm" point. Try it!

Did you know? Everything is controlled at the park, including sights, sounds and even smells. Disney pumps air into each "land" area to make sure the entire experience is immersive (meaning you are completely surrounded by it, so nothing from the outside world is there).

Kid's Tip!

Ask your parents to write down their cell phone numbers on something you won't lose (like your arm). You can show it to the Disney Cast Member if you get separated. They can call your parents for you!

Disneyland is Filled with Awesome Fun!

Playing at the Parks!

Final Hints for your Visit!
Things that Fright & Things that Excite!

Before you get to the theme parks, download the Play Disney Parks app. It opens up a whole new world of fun for you, which changes based on where you are! For instance, the app becomes a Galactic Datapad when you arrive at Star Wars: Galaxy's Edge in Disneyland Park. You can scan objects, listen in on communications and even translate what you're saying to an alien language. Try it in each land of each park to see what fun you can discover!

The parks have so much to do, we could never describe all of it. We're going to try, though! Here is a table that lists the total number of shows, rides and games. You can see that the Disneyland Park has the most to do, by far!

Shows and Rides

Park Name	Number of Shows	Total Rides
Disneyland	7	34
California Adventure	7	18

Parades

Park	Parade Name
Disneyland	Main Street Electrical Parade, 3:00 Parade, Mickey and Friends Cavalcade, Frozen Friends Cavalcade
California Adventure	Varies with Current Events

Note: Shows and parades vary with the season. Check the Disneyland App to see what will be available during your visit!

Shows

Here is a table that lists all the shows. Read through the names to decide which ones sound interesting.

Park	Show Name
Disneyland	Pixar Pals Dance Party Disneyland Band at Tomorrowland Flag Retreat Ceremony The Straw Hatters Disneyland Band at Main Street USA The Dapper Dans Main Street Piano Player Fantasy Faire The Bootstrappers Jambalaya Jazz Fantasmic!
California Adventure	Citizens of Buena Vista Street Five & Dime Disney's Junior Dance Party Jammin Chefs Guardians of the Galaxy: Awesome Dance Off! Avengers Assemble! Warriors of Wakanda: The Disciplines of the Dora Milaje Doctor Strange: Mysteries of the Mystic Arts The Amazing Spider-Man! Operation: Playtime! Featuring the Green Army Patrol World of Color Mariachi Divas

Final Hints for your Visit!

Relax and Chill!

If you go to a park early in the morning, plan to take a break in the afternoon when the weather is the hottest and the parks are the most crowded. This is the best time to go back to your hotel and play in the pool or take a cat nap.

When you return later in the afternoon, you can go on a lot of the rides again. It will be cooler and not as busy.

Some of the outdoor rides are really fun after it gets dark, like Big Thunder Mountain Railroad!

If you get tired, most of the parks have fun ways to rest your feet. At Disneyland, take the train around the park or hop aboard the Mark Twain River Boat. California Adventure has a great, big ferris wheel. Take in the views and enjoy a nice slow ride around the Pal-A-Round.

Stage Fright! *"Exit stage right!"*

Don't worry if you get nervous waiting in line for a ride and "chicken out" at the last second. This happens to a lot of us at any age! There are exits before you get on the any ride at Disney that you can take without having to hang your head in shame. Just remember that the rides aren't actually dangerous or really scary when you get on them. They're all super fun!

Motion Sickness!

Be careful about the rides you take right after eating. Some of them can make you feel sick, especially if you have a sensitive stomach. If you ever get car sick, this may be you. So, be careful with

If you can dream it, you can do it.

- Tom Fitzgerald, Disney Imagineer

the following rides if you're worried about getting motion sick.

Disneyland
- Astro Orbiter
- Big Thunder Mountain Railroad
- Dumbo the Flying Elephant
- Indiana Jones™ Adventure
- Mad Tea Party
- Matterhorn Bobsleds
- Millenium Falcon: Smugglers Run
- Roger Rabbit's Car Toon Spin
- Space Mountain
- Star Tours

California Adventure
- Golden Zephyr
- Grizzly River Run
- Guardians of the Galaxy — Mission: BREAKOUT!
- Incredicoaster
- Mater's Junkyard Jamboree
- Radiator Springs Racers
- Silly Symphony Swings
- Soarin' Around the World
- Toy Story Midway Mania!

Kid's Tip!

ROLLER COASTERS

If you don't know how much you like roller coasters, try Gadget's Go Coaster in Toontown at Disneyland first. It's not scary at all, and the ride is over in a jiffy! If you like that one, try another roller coaster that is just a bit more exciting, like Big Thunder Mountain Railroad. If you still love it, you are ready for the most intense coasters of them all, Space Mountain, Matterhorn Bobsleds and Incredicoaster!

If you decide to try something even more exciting, see if you can sit in the front car of the coaster. This is the most fun because you don't have anything in front of you! (Sitting in front is also a smoother experience. The cars in the rear of the coaster tend to bang you around!)

If you want to sit in front, just ask the Cast Member when you reach the ride. There is a special place to wait—just a little off to the side—and it usually only adds a couple minutes to your overall wait time!

Things that Fright & Things that Excite!

It can be hard to tell if something is real or fake. For instance, the mechanical animals in The Jungle Cruise look very real and can scare people. Even movies, especially the 3-D ones, can have stuff that pops out and spooks kids. Other creepy things you might see are animated monsters and villains.

There are some local live animals that hang out in the parks. It is rare that any of the wild animals will scare you.

Look for ducks, squirrels, rabbits, and birds. They can get very "friendly" as they search for food! If you are bothered by any of them, you can usually gently shoo them away and they will leave you alone. Just remember not to feed them.

Robotic Machines. Probably the spookiest thing at Disney are the robotic creatures, called <u>Audio-Animatronics</u>. This is a big word that Walt Disney made up. It means that they combine the voices and sounds ("audio") with the moving machines ("animated electronics") to look real. (When the parks started, this was still brand-new technology that Disney developed!)

Depending on the ride, you may see wild animals, bears, and even spiders. If these get too scary, just remember that nothing can actually get to you. It is all make believe! They are simply machines operated by computers. None of the scary creatures are real. You'll even laugh when you see Donald Duck's rear end in Philharmagic!

Films. Disney has the greatest film technology ever! The 4-D effects include creatures, like spiders, scents, and even mist. If these get too scary, you can just take off your special 3-D glasses or look away.

Themes. Some rides are scary just because of their themes. The Haunted Mansion sounds scary, doesn't it? The special effects that create the ghosts look very real!

But none of the rides are meant to be anything more than a lot of fun. You soon discover the pretend ghosts are just playing around and singing and want you to join in their fun!

Noises. There are instances of loud simulated gunfights, cannons, or commotion that can be frightening. Remember these noises are just that - sounds! What you hear isn't actually happening, so enjoy the moment knowing that you're safe!

Live-action Performances and Scary Characters. Some characters can be scary. For example, Darth Vader is a bad guy ("villain") and he is very big. Another big character is Chewbacca. Even Goofy frightens some kids. He is one of the tallest guys in Disneyland! Maleficent looks big and scary, but she doesn't hurt a fly. These Characters are all part of the Disney magic - they're fun to enjoy… even if they might not be smiling.

Stunts. All dangerous stunts are performed far away from the audience. You may see simulated (that means made to look real) disasters, explosions, smoke and flames - all of which are all make-believe using special effects. Instead of getting frightened, try to figure out how Disney makes it all happen.

Famous Photography Faces! Disney takes a picture of you on lots of their rides. These photographs are usually taken at the point when you are the most excited!

This might be at the very beginning, like on Incredicoaster, or closer to the end, like on Splash Mountain.

Here are a few things to look for on Disney attractions. You might be fearless and have a fun time on everything, but some kids like to know what to expect.

Motion	**Environment and Special Effects**
High speed	Dark tunnels
Fast spinning	Strobes and Laser effects
Fast take off and inverted loops (on a rollercoaster — especially Incredicoaster!)	Loud noises, including some screaming
Drops from tall heights (especially Mission: BREAKOUT!, Splash Mountain, and Matterhorn Bobsleds)	Simulated fights, including gunfights
	Dark rooms, tunnels, open space
	Small or confined areas

Getting Around: Disneyland Transportation

Color the Parking Lot Tram!

The Disneyland parks are pretty big, but they were designed so you can walk back and forth easily. The Disney hotels and even most of the other hotels in the area are also a really easy walk away!

Because of that, Disneyland only has a few transportation options: the monorail, parking trams, and parking shuttle buses.

Let your parents know they need to fold strollers before getting on a bus or tram. Help your parents with your little brothers and sisters. Be sure they are seated properly with an adult.

Remember, the line to park at the parking garage can be long. Tell your parents to try to get there an hour before park opening to give you time to get into the park for "rope drop."

You can help out in the morning with your younger siblings. Be sure to ask your parents how you can help!

Monorail

The monorail is part of the free transportation system at Disneyland. It provides a fast method of traveling between Downtown Disney and Disneyland Park.

There is only one monorail track that will take you on a large loop 2.5 miles and 13 minutes around Disneyland. It travels through Disney's Grand Californian Resort, Downtown Disney and then back to Tomorrowland inside of Disneyland!

Sadly, no monorail tracks were built to go to California Adventure.

The location of the Downtown Disney monorail station makes this a great option if you're staying at a Disney hotel or parking in one of the Downtown Disney-area garages.

Since the monorail actually drops you off inside of the park, you need a park ticket to get on the train!

> ### Kid's Trivia!
>
> Mono means "one" and, unlike most trains that have two tracks, this one runs on a single track. What makes it even more fun is that it travels on a railway that is high in the sky above everyone! Walt got the idea for this revolutionary transit system at the 1962 Seattle World's Fair.

There are three Mark VII (seven) monorail trains. The Monorail system only uses a 600-volt DC power source, so it emits no direct exhaust or pollutants into the atmosphere. Each train is identified by its color. The three colors are:

1	Red
2	Blue
3	Orange

Occasionally, one of the monorails is given a temporary "wrap" around its body, or it could be decorated with pictures to promote a recent movie release.

For a really neat experience, ask if you can ride in the front or *nose cone* of the monorail train with the pilot. (You can only do this at Disneyland, not Walt Disney World!)

Disney Trams

Disneyland has two separate parking garages near the park, called Mickey & Friends and Pixar Pals.

Disney has a type of open-air bus called a tram. You can hop on a tram from either parking garage. It will drop you off near the main theme park entrances.

Disney Shuttle Buses

In addition to the parking garages, Disneyland has a separate parking lot, named Toy Story.

It's a little farther away from the parks (about a mile), but it's really convenient. That's because there is usually lots of parking available and Disney provides Shuttle Buses to the park entrances from the Toy Story lot.

Shuttles pick you up near your car and drop you off near the two theme park entrances. What a great way to travel!

Other Area Options

The city of Anaheim has an entire resort district. It's an entire neighborhood for tourists to enjoy, and Disneyland is just one part of that!

Anaheim has a whole bus transportation system set up to help you get around to all the hotels, restaurants, and even the convention center. It's called ART (Anaheim Resort Transit).

You and your parents can look at the bus routes and cost to use this bus system here: https://rideart.org/

Just remember, if your hotel is close to Disneyland, it's often faster to walk than take a bus. That's because the bus usually makes several stops between your hotel and the Disney parks.

You may have heard of taxi cabs or rideshare companies like Uber and Lyft. Those options are also available to drive you around Anaheim. Just remember, they can be expensive, especially during busy times of day.

Getting Around: Disneyland Transportation

Kid's Tip!

Younger kids want to visit Disneyland Park over any other park. It has the most rides and was all made just for kids to enjoy with their entire family!

Kid's Tip!

Ask for some pixie dust at the Bibbidi Bobbidi Boutique. They'll give you a fresh sprinkling of it over your head!

Color Sleeping Beauty's Castle!

Let's Go to Disneyland Park

Introduction to Disneyland

> Disneyland Park has the most to do and is the most fun for younger kids!
> More!
> More rides!
> More shows!
> More parades!

You don't have to be a kid to love Disneyland. Your parents and grandparents will love all it has to offer, too. It's full of enchantment! It's where you find thrilling rides, amazing entertainment, spectacular parades and magical nighttime fireworks shows.

Throughout the entire park, there are more than 50 attractions - that's a lot! In the table at the end of this section, we list the top attractions you are going to want to consider for your family's agenda.

Opening Ceremony

Arrive at the park first thing in the morning to catch its Opening Ceremony where Mickey Mouse and all his friends greet their guests with a fabulous show at the Main Street Railroad Station.

It's located just inside the park entrance.

Nine Lands of the Magic Kingdom

Sleeping Beauty's Castle is located "smack dab-in-the-middle" of Disneyland.

The Castle is surrounded by nine very different, themed areas, called *lands*. Each land is special in its own way and designed to transport you to a different time or place:

1. See lots of fun woodland animals and take a walk through the backwoods of Critter Country.
2. See the 19th century Wild West in Frontierland.
3. Experience turn-of-the-century Americana in Main Street, U.S.A. (based on Walt's home town).
4. Go way back in time to medieval Europe in Fantasyland.

Let's Go to Disneyland Park

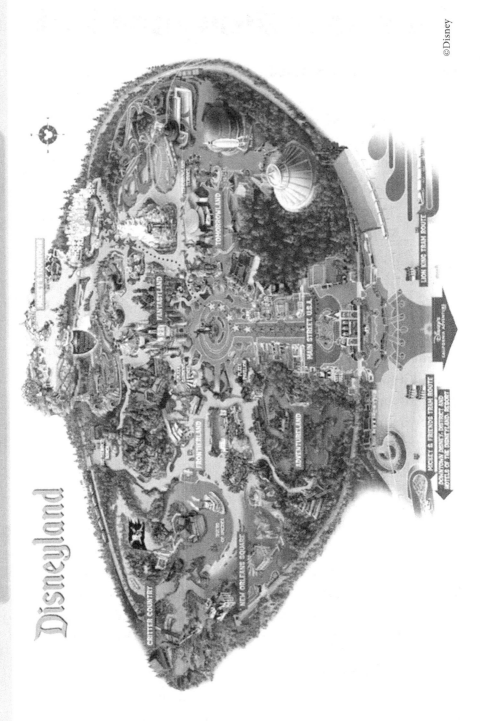

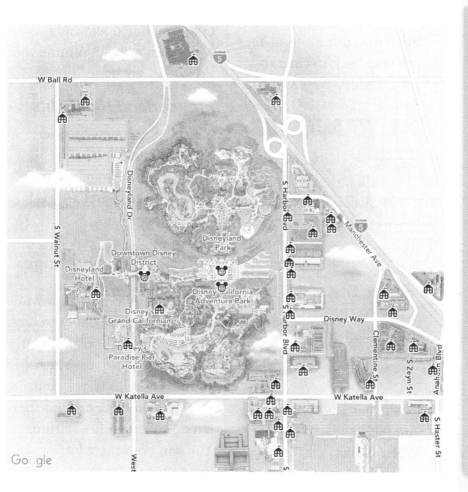

5. Have a timeless adventure through the Adventureland jungles.
6. Tomorrowland lets you travel at warp speed on a spaceship far into the future.
7. Take in the jazz music and smell of southern food as you step back in time to 18th century New Orleans Square.

Kids, Look up!

Hunt for weathervanes as you walk around the park. Look for the following ones:
- Rooster
- Moose
- Elf-like Troll with a Long Nose
- Crocodile

Do you spot others?

8. Grab your Lightsabers and head to Batuu in Star Wars: Galaxy's Edge to aid the resistance in their quest to take out the Empire.
9. Transport yourself into a cartoon world in Toontown.

Critter Country Highlights

Relax next to waterfalls and enjoy your lunch in the most peaceful area in the park. Keep an eye out for cute ducks and turtles in the Rivers of America. You can also take a plunge down Splash Mountain or help Winnie the Pooh find his honey pot.

Frontierland Highlights

Explore the new frontier: Big Thunder Mountain Railroad and Pirate's Lair on Tom Sawyer Island are each rootin'-tootin' fun!

Main Street U.S.A Highlights

Old-fashioned, small town fun is what this tribute to Walt's childhood is all about. Visit souvenir shops, a real train station (to travel on a steam locomotive around the park), and see a fire station. You can even meet lots of great characters (especially Mickey and Pals). Don't miss the Evening Flag Retreat, a special ceremony that salutes America.

Kid's Trivia!

Roy Disney was a U.S. military veteran. He served in the U.S. Navy from 1917 to 1919.

Walt wanted to join, but he was too young to enlist during World War I and too old during World War II!

He found other ways to show his pride in America, including volunteering for the Red Cross Ambulance Corps and drawing patriotic cartoons for soldiers and civilians to enjoy.

Flag Lowering Ceremony. The Disney brothers were great *patriots* (meaning they loved and respected their home country, the United States of America). They wanted to show proper respect to their country and its military members at the American Disney parks.

Most towns have a city hall where the U.S. flag is raised at the beginning of the day. At Walt Disney, only Cast Members are at work early in the morning when the flag is raised each sunrise.

Each evening, the flag is lowered during a Flag Retreat (flag lowering) ceremony. During the ceremony, there is a proper showing of respect to United States active military and veterans. (Veterans are people who served in the military.) During this performance, Walt Disney's Main Street Band plays patriotic music, including the American National Anthem, *The Star Spangled Banner*.

Tomorrowland Highlights

Futuristic rides zip you through the galaxy. Enjoy Buzz Lightyear's Astro Blasters and Space Mountain (Mega Thrill!).

Adventureland Highlights

Channel into your inner wild animal on the Jungle Cruise and sing along with the birds in the Enchanted Tiki Room.

Adventureland is the most exotic place you can imagine, just like Hawaii or the South Pacific.

Fantasyland Highlights

Story books come to life as you experience Peter Pan's Flight, Dumbo the Flying Elephant, Matterhorn Bobsleds (Popular Ride!), Alice in Wonderland, it's a small world, and Mad Tea Party.

Fantasyland, set in old Europe, is the most classic and popular land. It's the place most people think of when imagining a trip to Disneyland.

In this land, you become part of the story and get to live the whimsical world of Disney fairy tales.

New Orleans Square Highlights

Listen to the sweet sound of jazz music and smell those fresh beignets. New Orleans Square takes you back to the simple times when music and southern food fed the soul. Explore the great unknown on Pirates of the Caribbean or pick up some hitch hiking ghosts at the Haunted Mansion.

Star Wars: Galaxy's Edge Highlights

Transport yourself to a different planet with 3 suns! There's much to do here in Batuu. You can build Lightsabers and Droids or shop at the Outpost. Try some yummy frozen Blue or Green milk or boogie down at Olgas Cantina while you sip on an out of this world sweet drink. Join the resistance on Star Wars: Rise of the Resistance or fly the fastest ship in the galaxy on the Millenium Falcon: Smugglers Run.

Toontown Highlights

See where Mickey, Goofy, Donald Duck and Minnie Mouse live. This cartoon area has lots of play areas, picture props and some great rides!

Main Street, U.S.A.

This is a small, turn-of-the-century American town, set around the year 1900. In fact, Walt Disney designed Main Street to look a lot like Marceline, Missouri, the town where he grew up. Be sure to notice the street lights - they look like old-fashioned lamp posts!

In most early towns, the City Hall would be located within a couple of blocks of the Fire Department. Haberdasheries (That's a fancy name for a men's clothing store,

---

Every day, flag lowering ceremonies happen across the nation, especially where the United States has its military stationed. Every military base lowers the flag (near dusk) while playing the National Anthem. (This song is actually broadcast from all the overhead public announcement systems on military bases. Anyone walking – or driving! – has to stop what they are doing to show respect.)

Please Show Proper Respect. If you see the flag being lowered, or hear the National Anthem, the proper way to act is to **stop moving and talking**. If you are American, face the flag and put your right hand over your heart until the anthem stops. During the song, the flag is lowered, folded and taken away. (If you are wearing a hat, you may salute the flag instead, which is how most former-military members show respect.) If you are not American, simply stand quietly until the ceremony is over.

Disney Animated Movies

```
T O N A A M R R C E L L A O
O I A I E B N D N R O S P C
I H L K O B A N I S R R E I
A C A O D R L E S E O A T N
N C D O I O U I R L B C E D
S O D B N T M B E U I A R E
D N I E O H T M T C N C P R
E I N L S E A A S R H F A E
L P T G A R R B N E O O N L
G M L N U B Z I O H O A E L
N O O U R E A T M E D A S A
A A B J U A N O B M U D M A
T A D C L R A I S A T N A F
L U B T S W A L L E R B L E
```

WALL-E
PETER PAN
TARZAN
BAMBI
BROTHER BEAR
ROBIN HOOD
CARS
JUNGLE BOOK
PINOCCHIO
TANGLED
BOLT
MULAN
MONSTERS INC
CINDERELLA
ALADDIN
HERCULES
DUMBO
FANTASIA
DINOSAUR

but they also sell women and kids clothing at the Magic Kingdom's stores!), food service and other neighborhood businesses would be found close together. At Disneyland, the movie theater and restaurants are located across from city offices.

Main Street, U.S.A. is a great place to shop. You can find clothes, toys, balloons, souvenirs and candy! If you need a new embroidered hat (stitched with your name), there are many options at the shop called *The Mad Hatter*.

Meals and Treats. Main Street is also the place to fill bellies with a hot meal and drool over sweet treats: hot cocoa, ice cream, chocolate and candies galore!

Transportation around Town. A long time ago, before cars were invented, horse-drawn trolleys were used to help people get around town. If you show up early in the day, you can see real horses and even hop aboard the omnibus for a trip down Main Street. (You will learn more about these forms of transportation in a bit.)

Meet Characters. There are several places in Main Street, and throughout the rest of the park, to meet your favorite characters.

Claim your parade or show viewing spot! Go early to get the best viewing locations on Main Street to watch a parade or street performance!

Disneyland Railroad. The very first attraction in the park is on Main Street. It's a real locomotive train! You can board the train and journey around the entire park. Don't forget that Walt Disney loved trains. Look around the station for tributes to him.

Window Designs. At the front of each shop are classic window decorations. This was common to downtown businesses so people walking by the store could see what services or products the business owner (called a "proprietor") sold.

Business from Home. Look up to the second floor windows. Many years ago, downtown businesses often had an upstairs apartment where the business owner and his family lived. When the business owner was not busy, he would spend his time upstairs with his family. When he got busy, his wife and older kids could help run the shop.

Second Floor Windows. Second floor windows are really special on Main Street. The names of people written on them are real. Many are Disney Legends who helped build the parks!

> Shopkeepers often owned their own business and sometimes lived above their shop, on the second floor. (Otherwise, the second floor might be used for storage or offices.)

Sleeping Beauty's Castle. Sleeping Beauty's Castle towers above everything down at the end of the Main Street. When you reach the end of the road, you enter what is called forecourt plaza or *The Hub*. This is a great central meeting place if your family decides to split up.

Why is it called The Hub? The center of a wheel is called a hub and is used here because the park is laid out like a wheel. The Hub lies at the center and each "spoke" represents a path that leads to one of the six different lands. The "wheel" is represented by the train and pathway that goes all around the park.

You can either stroll around the park in a circular path, or choose to make your way back to Sleeping Beauty's Castle to easily take a new path to discover each land.

Historical Note: In old American towns, spires from the town church hovered high overhead, owing to personal beliefs that sustained the homesteaders. Citizens of Europe more commonly saw castle towers, which represented government and safety.

Church Bells Toll. It was common for cities to respect the end of the "work day" and ring their bells precisely at 5:00 pm. Even if the church was not near the center of downtown, it could still be seen (and heard) from a short distance away. At Disneyland, a somber civil ceremony takes place each day at 4:30 pm to mark the end of the day.

Disneyland Attractions

Main Street, U.S.A.

Disneyland Railroad

Walt Disney loved trains growing up. Walt and Roy had an uncle who was a train conductor. Their uncle would blow his horn every time he

> **Hidden Mickey Alert!**
>
> Check out the rock behind the Bathing Elephants... Do you see it?

passed through town, letting both of the boys know they were being thought about from far off in the distance.

Train Backstory. Did you know that when Walt grew up and could finally afford it, he had a real miniature train set up in the backyard of his home? It was big enough for his guests to ride aboard. (Walt was the locomotive engineer!)

Disneyland Railroad. Walt's love of trains meant he absolutely had to have trains in his parks. Train tracks circle the entire park for families to enjoy. It is a fun way to get around in style, and it gives you a break when your feet get sore or your legs get tired.

Carolwood Pacific Railroad was the name Walt gave to the 1/8th scale steam train and railroad he operated. (Look for pictures of him with his train near the stroller rental counter as you enter the park.)

Train Stations. Besides the station at Main Street, U.S.A., there are three other stations, one at New Orleans Square and the others at Tomorrowland and Toontown. You can get on and off at these other stations, so it's a great way to travel!

> *Kid's Review!* We really love the 18-minute journey all the way around the park. During the trip there are a few things to see, including Primeval World — Land of the Dinosaurs!

Locomotives. All five of the steam-powered train engines are about 100 years old! The four locomotives are named the C.K. Holliday, E.P. Ripley, Ernest Marsh, Fred Gurley and Ward Kimball. Look up these names to find out a little about each. (Hint: All except Mr. Kimball were legends in the train business. Mr. Kimball was an animator who helped inspire Walt's love of trains!)

Kid's Tip!

If you sit in the back row of the very last train car, the Conductor just might ask you to yell "All Aboard!" into the microphone!

Kid's Tip!

During your journey, the conductor tells you fun facts about the park. It's fun and you stay in the shade, which is perfect when it gets hot outside!

Main Street Vehicles

If you visit Disneyland early in the day, you just might see one or more of the following classic vehicles.

- Horse-drawn street car, an old-fashioned trolley pulled by a horse
- Jitney, an early automobile with no roof
- Fire Engine, a replica of the earliest fire truck
- Omnibus, a gas-powered, open-air, two-story bus

Not all of these vehicles are used every day. Stop by City Hall in Town Square to find out their schedule on the day you visit.

Grab a family member or friend and hop aboard a vehicle for a one-way trip up or down Main Street. The journey takes you between Town Square (at the front of the park) and the Central Plaza in front of Sleeping Beauty's Castle ("forecourt").

Fortune Teller Esmeralda. Esmeralda the Fortune Teller is located in the Penny Arcade on Main Street, just put a quarter in the machine and out pops your fortune card that predicts your future!

Maybe your future has a Churro in it!

Main Street Cinema

When your feet start to get really tired, head over to the Main Street Cinema to watch a fun 6–8 minute cartoon short.

What's a cartoon short? It's a short cartoon that was designed to play before a full-length movie starts.

The Main Street Cinema has 6 different movie screens with 6 different movie shorts including:

- Steamboat Willie
- Plane Crazy
- The Moose Hunt
- Traffic Troubles
- The Dognapper
- Mickey's Polo Team

These movie shorts date all the way back to 1928 when Walt first started getting into the film business. In fact, Steamboat Willie is the movie short that made Mickey Mouse famous!

Did you know? The earliest bus was enclosed and horse-drawn and is also called a horsebus. Omnibus has the Latin base "omni" that means "for all" so this means any type of vehicle used to transport multiple passengers. At Disney, the word omnibus means one that is engine-powered. The word "bus" is short for omnibus.

The Disney Gallery

The Disney Gallery is located on Main Street in Disneyland. You can see rare models, artwork and memorabilia from different Disney rides and movies on display.

Disneyana is the shop located next to the Gallery. It contains more artwork from your favorite movie scenes and characters. You can buy artwork to take home here, including works by famous Disney artists such as Thomas Kinkade.

If you're lucky you might wander in when there is a real Disney artist sitting at the drawing table, drawing up some of Disney's classic characters.

The Disneyland Story Presenting Geat Moments with Mr. Lincoln

If you're into both American and Disney history, don't miss this attraction! It combines a show and memorabilia gallery, making it the perfect place to rest your feet and get out of the heat for a bit, while learning some really cool things.

The show starts out with a short film of where President Abraham Lincoln was born and goes all the way up to when he was elected as president. You can watch Mr. Lincoln take center stage as he gives one of his greatest speeches.

Did you know? Abraham Lincoln was Walt Disney's favorite president. Both Disneyland and Walt Disney World have attractions featuring this president.

The first Audio-Animatronic version of Lincoln debuted in 1964 at the New York World's Fair and was so life-like that National Geographic magazine called the figure "alarming" in its realism. In 1965, the show moved to its permanent home at Disneyland.

KID'S TRIVIA!

The first Audio-Animatronic character that was ever created was Abraham Lincoln. You can see the original one that was used in the 1964 New York's World Fair at the *Walt Disney Presents* attraction in Disney World's Hollywood Studios.

After you watch the show, take a look around the Disney Gallery to see:
- A scale model of Disneyland Park from opening day on July 17, 1955
- A carousel horse from the Griffith Park Merry-Go-Round
- Rare illustrations, artifacts, artwork and models of attractions
- Behind-the-scenes photos of Walt Disney

- The short film Disneyland: The First 50 Magical Years, a nostalgic look at the park

Hidden Mickey Alert!

Check out the *Partners Statue*, a bronze statue of Walt Disney holding the hand of Mickey Mouse in the Castle Forecourt. Don't leave without a picture of this famous statue.

Hidden Mickey Alert!

Crossing the bridge from Main Street, U.S.A, look for a carving of Mickey's head in the tribal shields above the path.

Adventureland

The best way to picture Adventureland in your mind is to think of remote jungles in Africa, Asia, South America and the South Pacific. Think exotic adventure, lush vegetation, totem poles, congo drums, tribal masks—a land filled with undiscovered mysteries!

Jungle Cruise

Take a water voyage aboard a riverboat through the jungles of Asia and Africa. Be sure to keep an eye out for zebras, giraffes, hippopotamuses, lions, headhunters and more!

The boating adventure gets crowded throughout the day. Try to get here early in the morning or late in the evening for shorter lines. If you ride it after the fireworks, the evening journey is creepier! You can usually get a

Lightning Lane reservation for this ride to avoid long waits.

The *skipper* loves to tell corny jokes as he takes you on your boat ride. (The "skipper" is your boat captain and tour guide.) Try to remember as many jokes as you can. Which one is your favorite?

Adventureland Treehouse

Get excited to explore the Swiss Family Robinson's 80-foot tree house. Be prepared to move those legs—you go up and down 68 steps on different floors. But the climbing is worth it! Discover what life would be life if you living in a real tree house.

One of the coolest things about the tree house is the overhead view of Disneyland. As you are exploring and climbing, don't forget to snap some selfies from high above Adventureland.

You can't get Lightning Lane reservations for the tree house, and you don't need them. There's almost never a wait to enter.

The tall treehouse at Disneyland closely resembles the original one used in the film. This is a walking (really a "stair-stepping") attraction, which means you get to explore the treehouse at your own pace!

You can't get Lightning Lane reservations for the tree house, and you don't need them. There's almost never a wait to enter.

Guess what? The Adventureland Treehouse isn't built on a tree at all—the body is built with a strong, solid-steel structure to fully support all those people climbing up and down. The tree "roots" are made of concrete and steel bars that extend into the ground 42 feet. That is four-stories deep!

The carving looks so real, you would never guess that it's not a real tree. Its 6,000 leaves are made of vinyl and can withstand the winds and rain of California—these leaves never fall!

Excitement Factor! You get to climb a real tree house high in the sky!

> **KID'S TRIVIA!**
>
> Disneyland used to have Tarzan's Treehouse. They decided to go back to their "roots" and change it back to its original Swiss Family Robinson form.

Indiana Jones™ Adventure

Are you ready to be an explorer like Indiana Jones? If you dare venture into the Temple of the Forbidden Eye watch out for booby traps, molten hot lava, mummies, giant insects, collapsing bridges, snakes, spears and a massive boulder!

As you venture into the tomb in a rugged troop transport, hold on tight – this is a bumpy and dangerous ride! If you can make through this wild adventure, you're tougher than you think!

Hidden Fun! Hidden Fun! The fun starts in the queue line after you enter the Temple. Look for the room with the spikes, there's a bamboo stick on the left-hand side. If you shake the bamboo, the room will sound like its collapsing.

In the room with the rounded ceiling, look for a sign that says "danger, don't pull the rope" and pull the rope!

Walt Disney's Enchanted Tiki Room

Sing along with bird buddies José, Michael, Fritz and Pierre at this Audio-Animatronic show. These wisecracking birds love to tell funny jokes!

Guests have been singing "In the Tiki, Tiki, Tiki, Tiki, Tiki Room" for about 50 years, and the attraction exists

> "To create a land that would make this dream reality," said Walt Disney, "we pictured ourselves far from civilization, in the remote jungles of Asia and Africa."

at Disney World's Magic Kingdom, too!

In the Tiki Room, birds aren't the only ones that sing. The flowers sing too and the carved masks hanging in the wall actually move! The show takes place all around you. The loud thunderstorm at the end can spook some young kids - but remember, it's just pretend!

Adventureland is divided into two main areas: the Arabian Village and the Caribbean Plaza. This is home to the awesome ride that inspired a blockbuster movie series, *Pirates of the Caribbean*. (That's right - the ride came before the movies!)

Hidden Mickey Alert!

Look at the bird perches to spy a couple of Hidden Mickeys.

Frontierland

Have a real Wild West adventure! This could have been the most unlawful place in all of Disneyland, but a new sheriff named Woody is in town! Now it's just fun to explore Disney's Old West ghost town.

Kid's Trivia!

"Ghost town" doesn't mean a place is haunted. This term refers to a town from which everybody has moved away and left it abandoned. Lots of Old West towns became ghost towns during the gold rush of the 1800s. People moved in to mine the area, then left as soon as the gold ran out!

Kid's Trivia!

Note the building addresses in Frontierland. These numbers represent the year that each building style was common in the real West!

Frontierland Fun

There may not be a lot of rides in Frontierland, but kids love all the rootin-tootin fun things to do.

In fact, two of the three "Disney mountains" are either in or next to this land! You can travel on a runaway train through a haunted gold mine and get soggy wet on the best flume ride in the world within a few steps of each other!

> **KID'S TRIVIA!**
>
> As the West was won (meaning that it was explored and people built their homes and businesses), many small wilderness frontier towns were established. These towns had to be close enough in distance where horses could easily travel from one to the other in a single day. This usually meant that they were no more than about 20 miles apart. They sprung up everywhere, but none of these towns were ever as fun as the one at Disneyland.

Good vittles (this means food!) can be found at Rancho del Zocalo Restaurante. It has some of the best Southwest and Mexican eats anywhere. As a bonus, you can usually find fun, frontier games to play just outside the restaurant, on your way to Adventureland.

The Frontierland Shootin' Exposition is a laser-rifle firing range that lets you polish your shooting skills using lever-action long guns. There are dozens of targets in the nighttime scene of a western village.

Pirate's Lair on Tom Sawyer Island

Explore a real island and meet other kids! Most of us love taking a raft across the small river to the island where Tom Sawyer had a lot of fun when he was young. (He is the main character in The Adventures of Tom Sawyer book, written by Mark Twain. He was a big deal!)

Wandering wonderment! Wander down the paths and up the hills, while having fun running across a real rope bridge to Smuggler's Cove! After that, pretend you are a pirate and head over to explore the haunted caves of Dead Man's Grotto.

Imagine hiding out in each of the island's caves. Look for the secret pirate's treasure, hidden on the island.

Tom Sawyer Island is a pretty big area with a lot of paths to run down. Calm, tame and quieter than other places at Disneyland, it also has nicely shaded areas where your parents will appreciate relaxing while you run wild! Tom Sawyer Island is not open past dusk (when the sun goes down), so get there early in the day.

Kid's Tip!

If your parents grumble about being tired, but you have lots of energy, head to Tom Sawyer Island. You can play all you want while they relax!

Mark Twain Riverboat

Why not try a very rare experience, like floating around the river on a real sternwheel paddle boat, just like those that traveled the mighty Mississippi River? (The stern is the back of the boat, which is where the waterwheel is located.)

The Mark Twain Riverboat is an authentic replica of a 19th-century paddle wheel riverboat. Chill out on a 15- to 20-minute river cruise around the Rivers of America waterway (the river that circles Tom Sawyer Island).

Look for her boarding station at the covered dock, located across from Big Thunder Mountain Railroad and The Golden Horseshoe.

Claim a spot up front if you want to take a lot of great pictures, or stand in the back where you can see along both sides of the boat. Not only is the trip excellent, there are cool sights that can only be seen by taking this journey.

Although the Mark Twain is very large—she holds up to 300 guests!—there are not a lot of seats, so you might have to stand when it's busy.

Sailing Ship Columbia

The Mark Twain Riverboat shares a boarding station with another ship, only this one will make you want to go fight pirates!

Cruise around Tom Sawyer Island on the Columbia. It's a 110-foot-long replica of an 18th century ship that once sailed around the world!

Explore the ship's cannons and its deck-mounted guns. These are what the old crews would use to keep the pesky pirates away.

The ship sails around the Rivers of America. Be sure to waive to the guests on land!

Did you know? It took the real Columbia ship three whole years to sail around the world!

Big Thunder Mountain Railroad

Not all kids love roller coasters, but those who do think this one is excellent! It is called, "The Wildest Ride in the Wilderness!"

The scene is set in an old, deserted gold mining town. Cursed runaway mine trains take you up and over the mountain top and through the town at breakneck speeds! Notice all the awesome scenery that looks just like a real working gold mine did over a hundred years ago! Keep an eye out for chickens, donkeys, goats and other animals. Did you see the poor, old man soaking in his outdoor bathtub?

Disney lovers know about the three "mountains" in Disneyland: Space Mountain, Splash Mountain and Big Thunder Mountain Railroad.

Did you know there's actually a fourth mountain? That's right! Matterhorn Bobsleds may not have the word "mountain" in its name, but it's one of the biggest mountains in the park!

These are all wild rides and not for the faint of heart!

> **Kid's Tip!**
>
> Big Thunder feels different at night than it does during the day. Try to go on it early and then right before you go home, after dark.

HELPFUL HINT: This tame ride is a good test to see what to expect on even bigger roller coasters! If you are at all nervous, go on Big Thunder Mountain Railroad before you try Space Mountain.

There are not too many abrupt dips on Big Thunder Mountain Railroad. If you're going up a large hill, expect you'll be riding back down! There are a few fun rolling hills and fast turns!

Sharp turns may scare some kids, especially if they get squished from a bigger kid or adult sitting next to them! The lap bar only drops down to the highest lap. For this reason, try to sit with another kid, or you might feel yourself fly around a little bit too much. It can be thrilling and a little scary if you feel like you might fall out, but you won't!

Minimum Height Required: 40" tall (3 feet, 4 inches)

> **Hidden Mickey Alert!**
>
> When you exit the ride, look for a prickly cactus with a familiar shape.

Frontierland Shootin' Exposition

Howdy pardner! Take aim and test your frontier shooting skills with a replica .54-caliber Hawkins buffalo rifle.

Special surprises await when you and other sharp-shooting bandits hit your targets in this Wild West-themed shooting arcade. It's so much fun!

(There's a small fee to play this gaem. Ask your parents for a couple of dollars if you want to shoot some varmints!)

Critter Country

Critter Country was originally named Bear Country. It was themed after the forests of the Pacific Northwest. (Can you name all

Kid's Trivia!

Why is Splash Mountain called a flume ride? In the old days, before big trucks were available to haul timber (trees), woodsmen used to move logs down the mountain using water flumes along rivers and lakes. This is what inspired today's theme park log rides.

nice place to rest, this area is the best to put your feet up and take a breather. You or your siblings can even take a quick cat nap!

Splash Mountain

  You're going to love this ride. It is almost everyone's favorite for thrills!

Follow the exploits of Br'er Rabbit as he runs away from home and tries to stay away from Br'er Fox and Br'er Bear. The scenes come right from Disney's 1946 film, Song of the South. (That is over 70 years ago, if you do the math!)

As Br'er Rabbit goes through the exit at the end of the story, you drop with him down a tall waterfall. It's impossible to guarantee you'll stay dry. Expect to get a little wet, and there is a chance you might get a bit drenched!!!

Kid's Tip!

The front, right side tends to get you the wettest, but the first rows always get drenched - try the left seat, back row if you want to stay slightly drier OR request to sit in the front to get soaked!

There are three small hill drops inside the ride. One last, slow uphill trip takes you to the final big splashdown to the bottom of the mountain.

Hidden Mickey Alert!

In the final scene after the waterfall plunge, look for a sleeping Mickey high in the clouds.

Remember to smile, because your picture is taken just as the log starts to drop! Try to keep your eyes open for the picture before you squeeze them closed for the landing!

Minimum Height Required: 40" tall (3 feet, 4 inches)

HINT: Get a Lightning Lane reservation if this is important to get into your schedule!

The Many Adventures of Winnie the Pooh

The fun starts before you even get on this ride! Imagineers created a really fun interactive queue area with a kids-only journey through Pooh's house (a tree trunk). Play in a whimsical garden, steer the honey bees through a maze and wipe the Hunny Wall (*hunny* is how Pooh spells *honey*) to reveal hidden characters! (Be sure to wash your hands after touching the hunny walls!)

When you're ready to ride, hop aboard a giant Hunny Pot and travel through the pages of a Winnie the Pooh storybook. Adventure through the Hundred Acre Wood and help Pooh find his pots full of sticky, sweet honey.

Can you feel the howling winds and see the rustling and blowing leaves? These strong winds blow Piglet and Roo off their feet and threaten to blow Owl's treehouse away!

Kid's Trivia!

Dumbo the Flying Elephant is one of the original Disneyland attractions, meaning it was there within the first year that the park opened in 1955. Do you know all the original attractions that are still there?

- Autopia
- Casey Jr. Circus Train
- Disneyland Railroad
- Dumbo the Flying Elephant
- Golden Horseshoe Saloon
- "it's a small world!"
- Jungle Cruise
- King Arthur Carrousel
- Mad Tea Party
- Main Street Cinema
- Mark Twain Riverboat
- Mr. Toad's Wild Ride
- Peter Pan's Flight
- Snow White's Enchanted Wish (called Snow White and the Seven Dwarfs)
- Storybook Land Canal Boats

Have you always wanted to bounce with Tigger? Everyone gets in on the fun, because the whole Hunny Pot goes up and down!

Throughout the ride, many more of Pooh's friends appear. Try to spot them all!

Oh, Bother! When Pooh wakes to realize it was all a terrible dream, he sees that it is raining outside and his honey pots might get washed away in a flood. But the ride ends happily. Pooh gets his honey back and all his friends shout hooray!

Davey Crockett's Explorer Canoes

Hop aboard a 20-person free floating canoe, with no motor and no track to guide you down the Rivers Of America!

Feel the wind in your hair as you paddle your way around Tom Sawyer Island, on one of these 35-foot-long canoes.

You and your family will paddle through 3 separate lands and pass several waterfalls, before returning to the dock. Don't forget to watch out for the ducks!

New Orleans Square

New Orleans Square connects Frontierland and Adventureland. It is mostly restaurants and shopping, but it is home to some of the best rides in the park. Check out the awesome ride that inspired a block-buster movie series, Pirates of the Caribbean. (That's right - the ride came before the movies!) It is also home to one of Disney's spookiest rides (but not really scary!): *The Haunted Mansion*.

The Haunted Mansion

The Haunted Mansion is a spooky (but not too scary) haunted house that claims to be "home to 999 ghosts." (They are always looking for one more!) Walt Disney himself wanted the attraction to be family-friendly, so there are lots of silly scenes along with mildly scary stuff, including many ghouls.

Be sure to read the headstones while waiting in line—they have funny sayings on them like "Here lies my snake whose fatal mistake was frightening the gardener who carried a rake."

You begin your haunted adventure in the funeral parlor. The whole group gets "locked" in the creepy room before realizing there are *no windows, no doors* and *no way to escape*! Suddenly, the room starts to stretch downward… shortly before becoming pitch black. (Don't worry, it's over in just a few seconds.)

Once you escape the parlor (whew!), board a *Doom Buggy* for a slow journey through the house, up to the attic and then outside and down to the graveyard.

As you travel inside the Haunted Mansion, your Doom Buggy takes you past a creepy book case full of ghost stories, an organ that plays by itself (look at the shadow on the floor!) and glowing footsteps. There are so many fun and slightly spooky sights, you may have to go again to spot them all!

Be on the lookout for freaky door knockers and a floating tea pot pouring tea for a ghost tea party. If you need a laugh, check out the dancing ghosts– try to spot the funny sleeping one under the table in the grand ballroom!

Famous hitchhiking ghosts catch up to you at the end of the ride. This is one of the highlights. Just wait until you see what fun tricks they have in store for you!

Attraction Reaction!

Scary... The ghost theme can scare kids (and some adults) - but only until they realize it's all good fun! The momentary darkness in the parlor room mentioned above makes some kids scream a little. Hold onto someone's hand and it won't be nearly as scary. And remember, it's all special effects and just meant to be a lot of silliness and laughs!

Kid's Tip!

There may be 999 happy haunts within the Mansion, but only 109 of them are Disney-created Audio-Animatronics! The rest are created with other types of special effects.

Pirates of the Caribbean

Pirates of the Caribbean may sound like a scary ride, but look a little deeper into the details and you realize it's clever and fun!

You begin your adventure by peacefully floating through the Bayou, while the sounds of crickets and banjo music fill the night air. (It's always nighttime on this attraction!)

One of the really cool features of this ride is that it starts by going past diners at the Blue Bayou restaurant! Wave to the people eating as you float past. They are on the right-hand side of the boat. On the left is a little wooden shack with fireflies lighting up the sky.

As you turn the corner, the ride gets really fun and spooky when you enter a pirate-ghost mist. Listen closely for an ominous warning. For younger kids, this may be a bit scary, so be sure to show your siblings a brave face – and hold on tight for the small drop, as your boat "slides" down into the bay! (Don't worry – this drop is easy compared to Splash Mountain. It's a little like an indoor roller coaster when it drops, but it's way more fun that frightening!)

The only kids who might be afraid of this part are a really young brother or sister who is afraid of the dark. Don't worry, though, the spooky part is over in a jiffy, and the rest of the ride is full of action, adventure and singing pirate songs! (If you are old enough to read this yourself, you are going to LOVE this ride!)

Excitement Factor!

Pirates of the Caribbean is an exciting ride with many Audio-Animatronic characters.

Look for the big pirate ship in the middle of the bay. *Watch out!* You're in the middle of the action as the pirates attack a small seaside village with lots of cannon fire! Don't worry, though. They aren't actual cannons!

The special effects just make it seem like the balls are really firing at you when the shots "hit" in the water a few feet away.

Flashes of light and blasts of air from beneath the water give the illusion of cannon balls being fired at you, but missing and landing in the water.

Did you know? This ride was around long before the movie series! The attraction has been a mainstay at Disneyland since it opened in 1967. The first of the movies, Pirates of the Caribbean: The Curse of the Black Pearl, didn't arrive at the theaters until 2003. How many years later is that?

The first movie took scenes right out of Disney's attraction! If you saw the movie, you are going to recognize many elements, such as the jail keeper's dog and pirate prisoners. Going full circle, Disney updated the ride after the movies became a huge hit. You now get to see Captain Jack Sparrow in odd places and situations throughout the attraction!

Later on, look for pirates looting and pillaging a village. There's a really fun scene where a lady is chasing an invading pirate with her broomstick!

Throughout your Caribbean Adventure, you get to sing along with the ever-familiar, "Yo Ho, Yo Ho, a Pirate's Life for Me!"

A SAD NOTE! Pirates of the Caribbean was the last Disneyland attraction for which Walt Disney oversaw the construction before he passed away.

Fortune Teller-Fortune Red

Head on over to Royal Street near Pieces of Eight and Pirates of the Caribbean and get your fortune told by an old scurvy pirate! Maybe he'll tell you if you'll find the hidden treasure.

Fantasyland

This is where the magic begins, just behind Sleeping Beauty's Castle! Some people call it "Storybook Central." Many Disney movies are represented here, including some of the best fairytales, such as Sleeping Beauty, Peter Pan, Pinocchio, Winnie the Pooh, Snow White and the Seven Dwarfs, and many others!

Fantasyland is the best land for kids!

All kids and even adults love visiting here. Because it's such a popular land, it becomes busy pretty early in the morning and many of the attractions quickly get long lines.

Kid's Tip!

The best time to visit Fantasyland is first thing in the morning or during the nighttime shows and fireworks (if you've already seen them!).

Sleeping Beauty's Castle Walkthrough

Take the winding pathways and stairs to the top of the tower and imagine life as a Disney prince or princess! This isn't a ride. Instead, colorful 3D displays show the tale of Princess Aurora, from her enchanted curse to finding true love.

Enjoy amazing artwork and scenes from the movie. Read the book and listen to the sounds and special effects that are designed to keep you on the edge of your seat (even though you're standing!).

Prepare yourself for the finale scene where Maleficent turns into a fire breathing dragon. Don't worry, Sleeping Beauty's prince charming comes to save the day!

Kid's Trivia!

- Sleeping Beauty's Castle was inspired by a real castle located in Bavaria, named Neuschwanstein castle. Read up on that castle's interesting history and the "Mad King Ludwig."
- This is the only Disney park castle that has a real, working drawbridge.

King Arthur Carrousel

The King Arthur Carrousel was one of the original Disneyland rides that was there on opening day, back in 1955. This carousel was handcrafted by the Dentzel Carousel Company in Philadelphia, Pennsylvania and eventually found its way to Sunnyside Beach Park in Toronto, Canada in 1922.

When Walt Disney first purchased this carousel, it featured horses, giraffes, deer and other animals. Walt wanted everyone to ride a horse just like King Arthur, so additional antique horses were added into the renovation.

Note: Disney spells the word carrousel in the title using an additional "r." This is an old-fashioned way to spell the word.

Each of the 68 hand-carved horses on the carousel is completely unique. Be sure to look up and notice the hand-painted scenes from Sleeping Beauty on the ceiling!

The carousel rotates to classic Disney tunes played from an old-fashioned fairground organ.

Mr. Toad's Wild Ride

Join Mr. Toad in a 2-person buggy on this wild ride. Discover why this is a classic Disneyland favorite!

Skid through the library and formal dining room, crash through the window and race past the riverbank. Stay on course and avoid being caught by the policemen, all while trying not to crash into a heaping stack of freshly baked pies!

Dodge the fiery explosions and look out for the train! How will you survive this crazy and fun ride?!

KID'S TRIVIA!

Mr. Toad's Wild Ride was once also found in Walt Disney World's Magic Kingdom. When Disney closed it there, they left a secret monument to Mr. Toad.

There's a pet cemetary near the exit of the Magic Kingdom's Haunted Mansion. In it is a special headstone just for Mr. Toad!

Alice in Wonderland

Take a ride down the winding, curving path as you enter the fantastical world of Wonderland. As you travel through the White Rabbit's House and the Queen's Garden, keep your eye out for The Mad Hatter, Tweedledee, Tweedledum and the Cheshire Cat.

Enjoy all the colorful scenes in your rush to make it to your "unbirthday" party!

KID'S TRIVIA!

You won't find this Alice in Wonderland ride in any other Disney park. it was made just for Disneyland's Fantasyland in 1958.

Mad Tea Party

The Mad Tea Party is a spinning teacup ride inspired by the Unbirthday Party scene in Disney's Alice in Wonderland. You get to ride in teacups, which rotate as they move around a huge, spinning platform. Each individual cup spins faster if you turn a big steering wheel in your lap.

Whirl 'round and 'round at a dizzying pace for about one and a half (1½) minutes (90 seconds). Look towards the center of the ride to see the mouse peek out from his giant teacup!

This fun ride can make some kids dizzy. Whatever

you do, don't go on this ride shortly after eating!

Kid's Tip!

If you start feeling sick on the ride, *focus on something on the horizon* (off in the distance) and *stop spinning the wheel*.

The Matterhorn Bobsleds

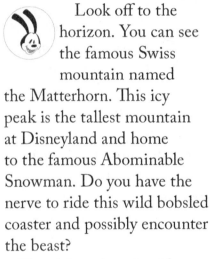

Look off to the horizon. You can see the famous Swiss mountain named the Matterhorn. This icy peak is the tallest mountain at Disneyland and home to the famous Abominable Snowman. Do you have the nerve to ride this wild bobsled coaster and possibly encounter the beast?

Your leisurely train ride through the snow-capped mountain soon becomes intense and fast-paced. It's quite a thrilling trip. Hang on to your hat as you travel through the dark, deep recesses of the mountain!

While racing through the mountain peaks, you just might catch a glimpse of the Abominable Snowman. Hold on tight (better yet, put your arms up!) as you encounter the large, fast drop down the side of the mountain.

Zipping along at top speeds, you might not catch all of the cool visual details. Try to keep your eyes open long enough to check out the caverns inside the mountain and the beautiful view of Fantasyland and Tomorrowland. Keep looking up while you race through the mountain, or you just may miss a face-to-face encounter with the giant and angry, ape-like creature.

Keep in mind there are a couple of intense jerks and sudden drops. This ride is wild, crazy, dark and scary! Are you brave enough to face your fears?!

Family members who don't meet the height requirements (or bravery requirements) can watch the crazy train riders zip down the mountain from just outside the ride (although it's way funner to experience it for yourself).

There are two bobsled tracks, one on the Fantasyland side of the mountain and one on the Tomorrowland side.

HINT: Try riding this attraction at night for a more thrilling experience.

KID'S TRIVIA!

- The original Abdominal Snowman resides with the collector over in Guardians of the Galaxy – Mission BREAKOUT!
- There is a small basketball court inside the Matterhorn.
- The Matterhorn used to have a hole in the top of the mountain through which a Gondola used to pass.

Minimum Height Required: 35" tall (2 feet, 11 inches)

Dumbo the Flying Elephant

 This fun attraction is based on Dumbo, the Disney film about the flying elephant. You will actually feel a bit like him, as you rise in the air and take flight above Fantasyland.

Dumbo is a short, two-minute ride. When you are on board, look for the lever that lets you control the up and down movement as you rotate in a big circle.

Typically, the lines are short early in the day and after dark when a lot of younger children start going home.

Small kids (3-8) love Dumbo! If you have a younger brother or sister, put this on your list of rides to experience with them.

Casey Jr. Circus Train

Are you ready to join the circus? Hop aboard the Casey Jr. Circus Train and take a trip through some of your favorite Disney villages, such as Arendelle from Frozen or London from Peter Pan. Your train travels high on the mountain for an elevated view of the miniature villages.

HINT: If you want a closer look at these miniature villages, get on the Storybook Land Canal Boats attraction.

> **KID'S TRIVIA!**
>
> Casey Jr. Circus Train was one of the original rides from when the park opened in 1955.

Storybook Land Canal Boats

Float in a 12-person boat through the hand-built cottages and towns of your favorite fantasy and Disney characters. These detailed models range from 1 inch up to 1 foot tall. See the familiar villages of:
- Arendelle and Elsa's ice palace- Frozen
- The straw, brick and stick houses- The Three Little Pigs
- London- Peter Pan
- Alpine Village- Pinocchio
- English Village- Alice and Wonderland
- Agrabah- Aladdin
- Prince Eric and Kingdom Tritons castles- The Little Mermaid
- The Dwarfs cottage- Snow White and the Seven Dwarfs
- French countryside village- Cinderella
- The Giants patchwork quilt- Lullaby Land
- Toad Hall- The Adventures of Ichabod and Mr. Toad

Peter Pan's Flight

Take off to Neverland with Wendy, Tinker Bell and Peter Pan! Peter Pan's Flight allows you to soar high into the nighttime skies of London in a flying pirate ship. Look for the tiny cars moving on the roads below. The ride is very smooth, as your fun flight takes off from the ground and soars high. (If you look closely, you can see that the track is actually up in the air - what the engineers call aerial).

Be on the lookout for Captain Hook and his dedicated sidekick, Mr. Smee. Also look for Tik Tok (the name of the crocodile that swallowed an alarm clock!) trying to catch the angry Captain Hook.

Peter Pan's Flight is amazing and fun; it's recommended for everybody!

HINT: Get a Lightning Lane reservation if you can. This

ride often has a really long wait time.

"it's a small world"

"it's a small world" is a timeless classic attraction, because it's been around since opening day of Disneyland. (It can also be found at Walt Disney World's Magic Kingdom.) You'll enjoy this relaxing boat ride as you travel through countries across the globe! This attraction celebrates people and cultures from all over the world. We learn that we are more alike than not.

KID'S TRIVIA!

"it's a small world" was built long before Disneyland. With the help of artist Mary Blair, Imagineers created the ride for the 1964 New York World's Fair. It was so popular, they had to put it in Disneyland and then in the Magic Kingdom when it opened in 1971.

See boys and girls wearing traditional clothing from their countries. They sing the theme song, *It's a Small World After All*, a few times over, sometimes in their own language! These doll figurines are mechanical and, though not technically Audio-Animatronics, still super fun to watch!

Look for the Japanese boy flying his kite, the Scottish bagpipers and even Polynesian hula dancers. Can you spot the jungle animals? Try to find hippos, monkeys and giraffes.

As you reach the end of the ride, the words "Good Bye" are written in languages from all over the world.

Spanish (Mexico)	Adios!
Hawaiian (Hawaii)	Aloha!
Japanese (Japan)	Sayonara!
French (France)	Au Revoir!
Italian (Italy)	Ciao!
Hebrew (Israel)	Shalom!
Danish (Denmark)	Farvel!
Chinese (China)	Zai Jian!

| Swahili (Africa) | Kwaheri! |

Did you know? The theme song is sung in five different languages during the ride. Over 100 countries are represented in total!

Hidden Mickey Alert!

When you get into Africa, look at the vines.

Pinocchio's Daring Journey

Hop aboard the woodcarver's cart and take a ride with Pinocchio, as he tries to escape the clutches of the puppet-master Stromboli. Will he give in to the temptations of Pleasure Island, or will his conscience guide him to safety?

Getting help along the way from his good buddy Jiminy Cricket, along with the beautiful Blue Fairy, join Pinocchio on his escape to the sea. Be extra careful, don't get eaten by Monstro the Whale!

Help Pinocchio find his way back to Geppetto and become a real boy, as Geppetto once wished upon a star.

KID'S TRIVIA!

"When You Wish Upon a Star" is the unofficial theme song for the Walt Disney Company. Can you sing all the words?

Snow White's Enchanted Wish

 Begin your journey with Snow White and the Seven Dwarfs in a wooden mine cart! Help Doc, Sleepy, Dopey, Grumpy, Sneezy, Happy and Bashful mine for sparkling gems. Watch out for the Evil Queen and help Snow White escape the Evil Queen's sorcery chamber to find her prince charming.

Is that fresh baked pie I smell?! Disney likes to pump different smells into their rides for a fun and yummy smelling experience.

The Evil Queen sometimes peers out of the window

above the entrance of the ride. If you're patient, you might get a glimpse of her.

Tomorrowland

Tomorrowland was designed with the future in mind! Imagineers wanted to show guests what the future may look like in the far-off year of 1986. It was designed back in 1955, but got a big upgrade in the 1990s. Tomorrowland features technology only dreamed of when it first opened (like rocket ships!).

Space Mountain

  This is one of the *most extreme roller coasters* in Disneyland. There are no inversions (meaning it doesn't go upside down), so it's not too scary. There are fast drops and sharp turns as you zoom around through the dark space. It is so dark inside that you can barely see where you are going, which adds to the fun. You don't need to see in order to hear the special sound effects of other rockets zooming around you.

Sit in the front of the rocket for the wildest ride! With no people in front of you, every dip and turn comes as a complete surprise. In the pitch black, it seems like you are moving really fast. While 28 miles per hour is *kind of fast*, it's not nearly as fast as other roller coasters you get to experience at Disneyland. For example, Big Thunder Mountain gets as fast as 35 miles per hour!

Space Mountain might not be good if you are afraid of the dark. The darkness can scare some kids, but it's totally worth it if you can overcome your fear!

Minimum Height Required: 44" tall (3 feet, 8 inches)

HINT: Get a Lightning Lane reservation or visit it first thing in the morning to avoid crowds.

Buzz Lightyear Astro Blasters

Your mission is to stop the evil Emperor Zurg! He has ordered his robot minions to steal all the batteries from all the friendly toys. They need the batteries to power their ultimate weapon of destruction.

As you board the ride, you enter into a real-life video game and play along with cartoon toys.

You might hear "To infinity and beyond!" more than once while you play.

Buzz drafts you into service as a Junior Space Ranger and you are under his direct command. Use your spinning spaceship to fight Zurg and his robots by firing at them with your laser cannon. A lever on your vehicle controls its movement, allowing you to spin left and right. The targets you want to hit have a big "Z" bulls-eye on them. Each time you hit them, you zap Zurg's energy and gain points.

Your score is recorded on the dashboard to compete against your family, friends, and other players. Top scores are posted on a big scoreboard at the end of the ride! Based on your final score, you are assigned a Ranger Rank.

If you are visiting during a busy time, get a Lightning Lane reservation. Otherwise, visit early in the morning or just keep an eye on the line toward the end of the day!

Kid's Tip!

To get the maximum points, hold the trigger button down the whole time. Aim for smaller and distant targets. They are worth more than larger ones.

Astro Orbiter

High above the middle of Tomorrowland is a spaceship ride called Astro Orbiter! It's above the glowing tower called Rockettower— you'll have to take an elevator up to the to the top of the building to reach the ride.

It's really cool to be able to look over all of Disneyland as you soar around colorful planets. This is a spin ride like Dumbo; however, it spins much more quickly! Also like Dumbo, there is a lever to control each ship's up and down movement. Sit in the front if you want the honors!

> *Kids' Warning!* This is a fast ride and kids with a fear of heights won't want to do it.

Be Nice! Please don't ever force someone to go on a ride that they're too scared to enjoy. That's not fun for anyone! Give encouragement. If that doesn't work, just let it go.

Finding Nemo Submarine Voyage

Put on your sonar hydrophones and join Nemo and his friends on this fun undersea expedition. Just like the Finding Nemo movie, you can help Marlin and Dory find Nemo!

As you dive into the ocean, keep a close eye out of the portholes and you just might encounter some friends from the movie such as: Bruce the Shark, Mr. Ray, Gill, Bubbles, Squirt and more!

Depending on where you sit in the submarine, your view will be slightly different every time. No matter where you sit, you will still be able to see and hear Nemo and his friends.

Autopia

In Tomorrowland, you can drive a real race car without a driver's license!

At Autopia, kids get to drive a gas-powered go-cart that is dressed up to look like an actual Hot Rod. That's right kids—YOU get to take the wheel! Take your parents for a drive for once!

You get to drive around a long, winding freeway in a car equipped with real steering and braking systems. Don't worry about crashing because the cars run on a metal guide rail that keep them on track. (Definition: A guide rail is a device or mechanism to direct products, vehicles or other objects through a roadway or rail system.)

Little kids love this ride! If your little brother or sister is too short to drive, take them on it for some quality racing time! Even if there is a long line, Autopia makes kids happy.

Minimum Height Required:

54" tall (4 feet, 6 inches) to drive the car by yourself;

32" (2 feet, 8 inches) to ride with a taller kid or adult

Star Wars Launch Bay

Do you love Star Wars? This building is home to some really awesome Star Wars things. Real and replica memorabilia from the movies are on display. You can even meet some of the characters. Be sure to get photos of everything, including the Cantina!

Explore every inch of the building – there's a special area with video games to play!

Star Tours – The Adventures Continue

This is a fun, 3D motion-simulated attraction that lets you fly through galaxies far, far away! You are in a spaceship rocketing through different Star Wars scenes on a mad dash to escape Darth Vader and the Dark Side.

The flight simulator has about 50 different scenarios, so each journey is vastly different and a complete surprise. C-3PO pilots your ship, and you may encounter many of your favorite characters, such as Princess Leia, Yoda, R2-D2 and even Darth Vader!

This is a bumpy ride that shakes you around. The wild ride has sharp turns and quick drops that seem very, very real.

Like all simulated attractions, don't eat anything before you board! If you begin to feel sick during the ride, close your eyes and it will get a bit better.

Minimum Height Required:
40" tall (3 feet, 4 inches)

Star Wars Galaxy's Edge

Walk around Batuu and shop at the Outpost, eat some out of this world food or even find some real-life Droids. Star Wars Galaxy's Edge features a real-life replica of the Millennium Flacon and several other fighter jets through out the land. Visit at night to see how the Millennium Falcon lights up

and to get photos with your Lightsabers!

Millennium Falcon: Smugglers Run

  Become a pilot, gunner or engineer, as you take a wild motion-simulated ride in the Millennium Falcon (Han Solo's spaceship from the *Star Wars* movies)!

Your mission is to retrieve supplies, but can you make it out with the ship in one piece?

Each ride is a bit unique, since you actually have some control over the ship's movements!

Minimum Height Required: 38" tall (3 feet, 2 inches)

Kid's Tip!

There's a secret "Chewie Mode" you can unlock on the *Millennium Falcon: Smugglers Run* attraction. Do a web search before your trip to find out how to do this special experience.

Star Wars: Rise of the Resistance

 Are you ready to join the resistance? Expect trouble during your first mission when a First Order Star Destroyer captures your transport.

Prepare to battle your way to freedom on this one-of-a-kind, multi-platform ride.

Minimum Height Required:
40" tall (3 feet, 4 inches)

Toontown

If you're feeling really goofy then Toontown is for you! Visit the Toontown jail, post office and even the homes of your favorite pals. Mickey Mouse, Minnie Mouse, Goofy and Donald Duck all have homes in Toontown that you can actually go inside of and experience life as a toon!

Take a tour and even get a photo and autograph with some favorite Disney friends. Toontown is also home to the exciting Mickey and Minnie Runaway Railway attraction!

Mickey & Minnie's Runaway Railway

Get ready for some silly fun when you board your train. Goofy is your conductor on this zany, action-packed ride.

When things go wrong, Mickey and Minnie race to save you. During your journey, dodge obstacles through twists and turns, and take a dance lesson with Daisy — all in your wild, trackless vehicle!

Chip 'n' Dale's GADGETcoaster

Climb aboard a wild roller coaster on your very own Rescue Ranger adventure with Gadget! Fly through the air, just like Zipper (the fly), as you soar high and swoop down low. This ride has tons of twists and turns that will leave you screaming for more!

It's a coaster meant especially for children, so the small cars are best for kids - but parents can certainly join in, too! Be sure to hang on tight! Even older kids love the speed!

Kid's Tip!

Who's who? For an easy way to remember the difference between everyone's favorite chipmunks, recall that Chip has a small black nose that looks like a chocolate chip! Dale likes to clown around. He has a big red nose, just like a clown, and a gap between his front teeth.

The ride starts out slow but picks up a lot of speed. It is fast and thrilling but ends quickly as it's only 30 seconds long; that's just a half minute! Because this is a really short ride, it's great for beginners to find out if they like roller coasters!

Donald's Duck Pond

Come see where Donald Duck lives! Climb up the spiral staircase to be captain of the boat. Don't forget to ring the bell and pull on the whistle to see water squirt up onto the boat's deck. Once you climb to the top, you will be able to look over all of Mickey's Toontown!

Goofy's How-to-Play Yard

Goofy's Playhouse is located right next to his best bud Donald's house. You can't miss it – just look for the goofiest house in Toontown!

With music-making slides and honey drips, it's the time of your life. Once inside, see Goofy's candy-making contraption, his crazy kitchen and where he hangs his hat after a long Goofy day!

Roger Rabbit's Car Toon Spin

Follow Roger Rabbit as he tries to save his loving wife Jessica Rabbit from the Weasels. Catch a ride in Benny, the cartoon taxicab. Together, race through town to try to save Jessica before it's too late.

Be careful not to slip and slide into too many things, or Benny may spin out of control. Your car can spin in a full circle – just keep turning the wheel as fast as you can!

Mickey's House and Meet Mickey

Take a tour through Mickey's house to see where the world's most famous mouse eats and sleeps. Try not to laugh too much at his messy bed when you walk through his bedroom – he's a very busy mouse!

In his downtime, Mickey enjoys watching TV in his living room with his lovable dog Pluto and baking in the kitchen with Donald and Goofy.

After your tour, take a minute to watch a short movie while waiting to meet Mickey Mouse himself. Before you know it, you'll be next in line to take a photo with the famous Mickey Mouse. Don't forget to give him a big hug!

Minnie's House

Take a tour through Minnie's house. It's said to be the cutest house in Toontown! Minnie's house is decorated in pinks and lavenders with hearts and flowers everwhere.

Minnie Mouse is very crafty; she loves to sew and paint, as you can tell from her craft room. When you reach Minnie's kitchen, explore the refrigerator and microwave for some interactive fun.

Once you are in Minnie's back yard, be sure to have some fun in her yard and take pictures in the pink and purple gazebo. If you're lucky, Minnie may be in the garden waiting to meet you!

CenTOONial Park

Parks are fun, and this is one of the funnest! Get in touch with your creative side and dream up a cartoon of your own, just like Walt Disney did as a kid!

There's even a dreaming tree. It's inspired by the real tree Mr. Disney sat under as a kid.

The best way to get creative is to have fun, though. There's a super fun water play area to help you cool off and get a little wild!

Entertainment

Shows, parades and other special events are listed in the Disneyland App and on informational boards throughout the parks. Just ask any Cast Member if you can't find what you're looking for!

Dapper Dans

Main Street's barbershop quartet is a singing group that you can find traveling up and down Main Street, U.S.A. They even have a bicycle made for four aboard which they sometimes perform!

Parades (Various)

Whether you catch an afternoon or evening parade, favorite Disney characters pass by on larger-than-life parade floats. Wave to Anna and Elsa and other *Frozen* characters, as well as Peter Pan, Ariel, Cinderella and so many more!

If you're lucky enough to catch a nighttime parade, such as the **Main Street Electrical**

Parade, the floats and characters light up the night!

Plan ahead and find a good spot to watch on the curb anywhere along the major roads (promenades) at least 30 minutes before the parade begins. Parades are so amazing that everyone wants to see it, and it's smart to find good spots really early.

This parade takes place once a day in the afternoon. (Check the Times Guide for exact parade times.)

Cosmic Dance Party

Can't get enough dancing? Check out the Cosmic Dance Party that occurs most nights at Rockettower Plaza Stage in Tomorrowland. (Keep in mind it's only open "weather-permitting" which means that if it rains, the show is canceled.)

Mickey's Mix Magic & Disney Enchantment Nighttime Shows

Scenes and songs from Disney movies take over Sleeping Beauty's Castle and the night sky above.

Mickey's Mix Magic is a projection show in which the castle comes to life with a dazzling display of projected scenes accompanied by the music you love.

Later in the evening, the **Disney Enchantment** fireworks show illuminates both the castle and the sky over Sleeping Beauty's Castle in the middle of the park! Lasers and projections play scenes of friendship and love all over the castle and down Main Street.

The best place to watch both shows is in the middle of Main Street facing toward the castle. Be sure to catch a glimpse of Tinker Bell flying from the castle to Tomorrowland!

Fantasmic!

The best way to end a day at Disneyland is to view the nightly fireworks spectacular starring Mickey Mouse in his biggest role of all time!

Fantasmic! is an entertaining show containing fun, technical elements such as water, lasers and lights, and of course, famous Disney characters! This show is set to a music soundtrack that every kid enjoys, your parents will remember many of these songs from when they were kids!

As the show begins, we enter Mickey's dream world. Disney villains show up to turn his dreams into nightmares. But don't worry too much, good always defeats evil, turning his dreams happy again!

This is a very popular show! The line starts forming at least an hour before the show begins. If you arrive late, you might not get a good seat. On busy days, you might not get into the show at all!

This is such a cool blend of live action, video, water ballet and fireworks. It plays most nights, often twice when the park is open late. The show is about 30 minutes long and is held on the Rivers of America.

The evening performances can get very chilly (except in summer). Certain parts of the show have pyrotechnics, so you might feel the heat from those displays (and get a little wet) if you sit close to the water!

Scenes from Fantasia, Cinderella, Mulan, Pinocchio, Dumbo, and many others appear before the audience on screens that are made out of water!

Character Meet & Greets

Meet a Disney Star

Even though you can see them in parades and shows, you can meet some favorite characters in person and get a photograph and autograph!

Character	Location
Goofy	Goofy's Playhouse
Mickey Mouse	Mickey's House (Toontown)
Minnie Mouse	Minnie's House (Toontown)
Tinker Bell	Pixie Hollow

*Available characters change regularly. Check the Disneyland App when you get to the park to see who is waiting to meet you that day!

KID'S TRIVIA!

Can you name all of the seven dwarfs?

1. Sleepy
2. Sneezy
3. Happy
4. Doc
5. Bashful
6. Grumpy
7. Dopey
8. Mickey

Wait a Minute! That list has EIGHT dwarfs on it! Did you read the entire list? If you did, you know that we added *Mickey* on the list of dwarfs. We know he is really a mouse and not really a dwarf. *We just wanted to have a little fun and see if you were paying attention!*

ATTRACTION RATINGS

Super Cool (MUST-SEE)	Cool (SHOULD SEE)	Fun (SEE IF YOU CAN)
Space Mountain	Jungle Cruise	it's a small world
Matterhorn Bobsleds	Autopia	Finding Nemo Submarine Voyage
Big Thunder Mountain Railroad	Tom Sawyer Island	Mark Twain Riverboat
Splash Mountain	Mad Tea Party	Tarzan's Treehouse
Indiana Jones Adventure	King Arthur Carrousel	Frontierland Shootin' Arcade
The Many Adventures of Winnie the Pooh	Roger Rabbit's Car Toon Spin	Walt Disney's Enchanted Tiki Room
The Haunted Mansion	Gadget's Go Coaster	Great Moments with Mr. Lincoln
Pirates of the Caribbean	Astro Orbiter	Disneyland Railroad
Buzz Lightyear Astro Blasters	Alice in Wonderland	Davy Crockett's Explorer Canoes
Star Wars: Rise of the Resistance	Mr. Toad's Wild Ride	Casey Jr. Circus Train
Star Tours - The Adventures Continue	Pinocchio's Daring Journey	Sleeping Beauty Castle Walkthrough
Millennium Falcon: Smugglers Run	Storybook Land Canal Boats	
Peter Pan's Flight	Snow White's Enchanted Wish	
Dumbo the Flying Elephant	Parades	
Fantasmic!		

Disney Princesses

Across
2. Don't mess with this princess who has been to war.
4. _____ White was the first Disney princess.
5. This princess dreams of a life on land.
7. She knows how to get down and dirty with a mop.
9. Don't cut her really long hair!

Down
1. She'll make you see the "Colors of the Wind."
3. The sea called out to this princess.
5. She met her true love and prince, before she even knew she was a princess.
6. The only way to her heart is through a library.
8. Only her sister, the Queen, could save her from a cold spell.

*Answers on Page 154

Let's Go to California Adventure!

Color Pixar Pier!

Highlights

The amazing Pixar Pier and Cars Lands are waiting for you to explore!

Take a fun scary elevator ride on *Guardians of the Galaxy — Mission: BREAKOUT!*

Go upside-down on the *Incredicoaster*!

Watch the Avengers battle bad guys.

Lights! Camera! Action!

Do you love *Toy Story*? Have you always wanted to meet a superhero?

California Adventure will take you into your favorite Disney and Pixar movies and make you part of the adventure!

Learn how to draw your favorite Disney characters at the *Animation Academy* in Hollywood Land. Go white water rafting on *Grizzly River Run*. Or explore the park's most popular lands: Pixar Pier and Cars Land.

©Disney

One section of California Adventure looks just like the city of Hollywood did back in its heyday (that means its prime years), when movies became really popular in the 1930s and 1940s.

Some of your favorite shows represented at this park include *Frozen*, *The Little Mermaid*, *Monsters, Inc.*, *The Incredibles*, *Toy Story* and *Cars*.

If you like wild rides, this park has two of the best: *Incredicoaster*, which turns you upside down, and *Guardians of the Galaxy - Mission: BREAKOUT!*, the most thrilling elevator ride in the world!

Since California Adventure is all about entertainment, the shows can't be beat; there are tons of shows throughout the day. There are also some of the most unique characters to meet, including the *Incredibles*, the toys from *Toy Story*, *Monster, Inc.* characters and the *Avengers*!

8 Lands of California Adventure

1. Shop and eat **Buena Vista Street**.
2. Take a walk down the streets of old time Hollywood in **Hollywood Land**.
3. Step into the life of a superhero in **Avengers Campus**.
4. Travel down Route 66 to Radiator Springs in **Cars Land**.
5. Enjoy lunch at an old fisherman's warehouse in **Pacific Wharf**.
6. Play boardwalk games on the **Pixar Pier**.
7. Enjoy live shows and entertainment in **Paradise Gardens Park**.
8. Enter the forest and rustic mountains of **Grizzly Peak**.

Buena Vista Street Highlights

Buena Vista street is made for shopping and taking in the sights! Take a stroll down and stop into the many shops filled with Disney toys and clothing. Enjoy caramel apples, cookies, cake pops and ice cream in one of the many sweet shops. You can even meet Mickey and friends near the fountain in the middle of Buena Vista Street.

Hollywood Land Highlights

Learn how to draw like a Disney animator, have a dance party with your Disney Junior friends and hang out with Crush, the turtle from *Finding Nemo*.

Avengers Campus Highlights

Watch your favorite heroes fight bad guys, help Spiderman sling webs at Spiderbots and help Rockets save his friends from the Collector.

When you're ready for a break, stop in to eat the tiniest micro foods or the biggest pretzel you've ever seen at Pym's Kitchen!

Cars Land Highlights

Learn how to dance with Luigi, swing with Mater and race with Lightening McQueen in Radiator Springs.

Pacific Wharf Highlights

Enjoy Chinese, Mexican and American food all in one spot. Don't forget to stop in for a massive ice cream sundae at Ghirardelli's. For a savory snack, take a quick tour through the bread factory and get a free sample.

Pixar Pier Highlights

Take a ride upside down on the Incredicoaster, or have a frozen treat from the Adorable Snowman.

Pixar Pier highlights

Find some awesome attractions inspired by your favorite Pixar films, like Toy Story, The Incredibles, Monsters, Inc. and Inside Out. You can also play really fun boardwalk games here!

Paradise Gardens Park Highlights

Enjoy live music during the evening, the World of Color at night, seasonal shows, activities and entertainment throughout the year.

Grizzly Peak Highlights

Take a stroll into the forest of Grizzly Peak, stop in for a wet ride down Grizzly River Run or burn some energy on the Redwood Creek Challenge Trail. (Your parents can rest in the shade on one of the many benches, while you play!)

The fan favorite Soarin' Around the World is also nearby. Glide over the wonders of the world.

California Adventure Attractions

Buena Vista Street Hub

Buena Vista Street is the hub of California Adventure. It resembles the old Los Angeles from back in the 1920s and 1930s. You will find lots of shopping and many places to stop and grab a treat!

Take your picture with the Storytellers statue of a young Walt Disney and Mickey Mouse. Don't forget to take a selfie in front on the Carthay Circle restaurant. The building was modelled after the famous theatre where Snow White and the Seven Dwarfs premiered in 1937.

Hollywood Land

Follow the old trolley tracks down Hollywood Boulevard and stop in the shops, eat a treat or step into the amazing Disney Animation building.

The Animation building has fun classes to teach you how to draw and animate your favorite Disney characters.

On the back streets of Hollywood, you'll find the live *Frozen* show, *Monsters, Inc. Mike & Sulley to the Rescue*, and many backdrops to take the coolest photos!

Mickey's PhilharMagic

Mickey's PhilharMagic is a four-dimensional (4-D) musical movie that appeals to all your senses! While there's so much to see and hear, you also get to smell tasty treats and feel a few puffs of air.

Enter the grand concert hall and put on 3-D glasses for this show. Be sure to look all around you—at one point, Donald Duck's Audio-Animatronic rear-end is sticking out of the back wall!

The majority of the show takes place on the huge theater screen. Mickey Mouse and Donald Duck are the stars while Ariel, Aladdin, Jasmine and Simba help to recreate some of the most beloved movie scenes—with a new twist!

Everyone in the family enjoys this fast-paced musical, while being entertained by the characters that pop out of the screen!

> ### Kid's Trivia!
> The name PhilharMagic is a play on the real word *philharmonic* which means that a bunch of musicians play their instruments together at the same time.

Monsters, Inc. Mike & Sulley to the Rescue!

Tour Monstropolis like a monster in this taxi ride through town. Listen and look for the emergency broadcast report as the ride begins. A human child is loose and must be captured! Help Mike and Sulley return Boo back to her door before she gets caught.

Red Car Trolly

Take a trip back in time and ride the vintage Red Car Trolly through Buena Vista Street. Wave at guests and pretend you've traveled back in time to Los Angeles in 1887. Back in those days, trolleys were a popular way to get around town. The Pacific Electric Railway trolly had more than 1,000 miles of track!

The Sorcerer's Workshop

Stroll over to the Sorcerer's Workshop and enter the Magic Mirror Realm. Discover the best animators' tips and tricks on how to make your still images appear to be in motion.

Look for the secret chamber in the Beast's library (Beauty and the Beast). Inside is an enchanted book that will help you discover which Disney character you are most like.

The Sorcerer's Workshop includes two exciting attractions: Animation Academy and Turtle Talk with Crush.

> **Did you know?** Mickey Mouse was not Walt Disney's first cartoon character. Oswald the Lucky Rabbit came first.
> The company Walt worked for owned the rights to use the character, so Walt had to create a new one. Oswald looks like he could be Mickey's longer-eared brother!

Animation Academy

Step out of the heat and into the cool air-conditioned building where you can learn how to draw your favorite Disney characters. At the Animation Academy you will get step by step instructions on how to draw, your own versions of some popular Disney characters. Classes start every 30 minutes! And the best part is, you get to keep your creation and take it home with you!

Turtle Talk with Crush

Turtle Talk with Crush is a totally tubular, live show where the cartoon character (from Finding Nemo) on the screen really talks to members of the audience. Even your parents are going to laugh hysterically!

Avengers Campus

There are several different shows that happen throughout the day in Avengers Campus. Watch your favorite superheroes including: Black Widow, Iron Man, Captain America, Thor and even the Black Panther.

You can also ride some of the most popular rides in the park, like *Guardians of the Galaxy — Mission: BREAKOUT!* After that adventure, help Spiderman sling webs at Spiderbots on the new *WEB SLINGERS: A Spider-Man Adventure.*

> **Did You Know?** You can go all the way through the queue and exit just before getting on any ride; it's often called using the "chicken elevator."
>
> Just ask to take the "chicken exit" before you get in the ride vehicle.
>
> A Cast Member will direct you to the exit. Try to be brave, though. We promise the rides are more fun than scary!

Guardians of the Galaxy — Mission: BREAKOUT!

The adventure begins when you enter the Collectors (Taneleer Tivan) private office, where he currently has the Guardian's of the Galaxy on display. Rocket soon breaks in and asks for your help to save his friends. Are you up to the task? All you need to do is hold up your hands for clearance once you are on the gantry (ride vehicle). Rocket will take it from there!

Buckle up tight! The gantry shoots up the shaft and drops back down in one of the wildest experiences of your life – all while listening to Peter Quill's favorite 80s music! As Rocket is working on breaking out the Guardians, you get to stop at each floor to watch them fight aliens and try to blast their way through the Collector's security.

Get ready to blast off! One final skyrocket to the top of the tower allows you to see all of California Adventure. (Of course, your photo is taken right as you drop!) Finally, the Guardian's have broken free all thanks to you and your bravery!

Handles are located in front of the seats if you need something to hold onto (other than Mom or Dad), but it's way more fun to throw your hands in the air! When you finish this ride, look for your photo in the PhotoPass area. There can be some really funny expressions on people's faces, especially yours!

Fun Fact! This ride was originally the Tower of Terror (just like the one if Disney World's Hollywood Studios).

Kid's Tip!

If you brave a ride on Mission: BREAKOUT!, make sure anything loose is secured. You don't want your change or snacks to fly around the car.

Kid's Tips!

- There's a special pocket for loose stuff (hats and sunglasses) in your car. Use it, so you don't lose something on this ride!
- In the Collector's office, find Peter Quill's Walkman and keep an eye on it as you are leaving. You will see Rockets paw reach down and grab it for Peter.

> **KID'S TRIVIA!**
>
> Even though it feels like you are free falling, you are actually falling faster than gravity. Disney Imagineers did not like how slow the gantry would fall on its own, so they set up a pulley system to give it super speed. There's one pulley at the top that lifts you up, and another pulley at the bottom that pulls you down at a whopping 39 mph!

Web Slingers: Spiderman Adventure

Are you ready to be a superhero? Help Spiderman shoot and sling spider webs at Spider-Bots that just won't stop replicating. The stakes are high. If you don't stop the Spider-Bots, they will start taking over the WEB Workshop, Avengers Campus and then the world!

Climb aboard the Web Slinger vehicle, put on your 3D glasses and get ready to sling some webs at Spider-Bots. Each Spider-Bot is worth points, some more than others. Try and sling a web as fast as you can!

Caution: Don't hit your sibling when flinging webs!

Cars Land

Take a stroll down Route 66 to Radiator Springs! Visit *Mater's Junkyard*, *Sally's Cozy Cone Motel*, *Flo's V8 Cafe* and *Ramone's House of Body Art*.

Make sure to stop and take a picture with the huge mountain range behind you. This 125-foot-tall replica is the largest rockwork created in a Disney theme park.

See who has the fastest car on the track on *Radiator Springs Racers*.

Don't forget to stop back in at night, when Route 66 is lit up with fun neon signs!

Radiator Springs Racers

Hop in a race car and start your tour with a relaxing ride on Route 66, all the way to the charming town of Radiator Springs. Speed on through, but watch out for Doc Hudson! Your buddy Mater will show you how to go tractor tipping and avoid being caught by Frank the Combine.

How about a shiny, new look before heading to the big race? Get brand new tires or a fresh paint job. When you're ready, line up for a quick start to the race. Hold on tight, the fastest car wins!

Luigi's Rollickin' Roadsters

Get ready to take dance lessons from the best dance teacher in town. Once you are in your 1950's car, Luigi teaches you to whirl and twirl to the Mambo Italiana and more. Try riding again for a different song and dance!

Mater's Junkyard Jamboree

Head over to Mater's place for a tractor hoe down. Hop into a tractor and hold on tight, as you swing and whip around the dance floor! This is a wild ride; these tractors really know how to shake it up boogie down.

If you're looking for Mater, check out the shed. Find him singing to his junky juke box, which is made from old car parts.

Pacific Wharf

When you're hungry, Pacific Wharf is the best place to go! This area looks like warehouse buildings in a local fishing area.

Eat at one of the many restaurants located there for lunch or dinner. The Pacific Warf has something for everyone to choose from. Even the pickiest of eaters will have an easy time finding something yummy to eat!

When you're ready to leave, toss a penny in the water as you cross the bridge and make a wish!

The Bakery Tour

Get ready to drool from the smell of fresh baking bread! Take a tour of a real bakery to see how Disney bakes their breads. The best part is you get a free sample of sourdough bread on your way out!

Pixar Pier

Pixar Pier features rides and treats from your favorite Pixar movies. Everyone thinks of Pixar Pier when they think of California Adventure. That's because one of the biggest and funnest roller coasters in any Disney park is there!

Help the Incredibles try and catch baby Jack-Jack on the *Incredicoaster*, try to outscore your brother or sister on *Toy Story Midway Mania!*, or take a ride on *Inside Out*.

Pixar Pier also has lots of boardwalk games to play and treats to try!

Games at Pixar Pier

Take a walk along the pier, and try your hand at some games of skill! There are four different games to play, all inspired by Pixar movies. Win the game and take home a prize! Or even better, win a prize for your younger sibling. (These games cost money, so ask your parents nicely if you want to play!)

La Luna Star Catcher

Try your best to nab a floating star at this family-friendly game. It's based on the animated short, La Luna.

Heimlich's Candy Corn Toss

Toss oversized candy corn into the mouth of the hungry caterpillar from A Bug's Life.

WALL·E Space Race

Aim a "fire extinguisher" to propel WALL·E and Eve higher and higher, as they twirl in space.

Bullseye Stallion Stampede

Roll balls into the right targets to make your horse run faster at this Skee-Ball game inspired by Toy Story 2.

Incredicoaster

Help the Incredibles catch baby Jack Jack, as the little tyke teleports from tunnel to tunnel, turns gooey and multiplies. Hang on tight! This high speed roller coaster shoots straight up and back down, around and even upside-down!

Don't forget to keep an eye out for baby Jack Jack in all the excitement. It will take the whole Incredible family and you to save the day!

There's a hidden Mickey on this ride, as you are going on the famous loop keep your head back and try to look at the ground. The pillars that hold up the ride form a hidden Mickey head at the bottom where they meet the concrete.

Jessie's Critter Carousel

Head on over to Jessie's Critter Carousel to rope yourself a critter from the Wild West. These cute desert critters will take you round and round, while you listen to some rootin-tootin country songs.

Inside Out Emotional Whirlwind

Take a ride inside Riley's mind with Joy, Sadness, Fear, Disgust and Anger in one of eight Memory Movers. Fly in a circle, up and down, all while you experience first-hand the Emotional Headquarters of Riley's mind.

Pixar Pal Around

You can't miss Pixar Pal Around. It's a giant Ferris Wheel with Mickey Mouse on it that towers over the park. This 150-foot Ferris Wheel gives you a great view of all of California Adventure from the top.

There are two queues for this Ferris Wheel ride. Choose wisely! One takes you to a typical Ferris Wheel gondola that stays in place, while the wheel goes round and round. The other side has a swinging gondola that moves and swings, as the Ferris Wheel goes around, giving you an extra thrill!

There are only two Ferris Wheels in the United States that have the combined

stationary and swinging gondolas. One is the Pixar Pal Around at California Adventure, and the other is the Wonder Wheel at New York's Coney Island.

Toy Story Midway Mania!

Shrink down to the size of a toy and help test out of all Andy's new shooting gallery games. This ride is a real blast! If you read about Buzz Lightyear's Spin in Disneyland and thought it sounded cool, this ride is even more awesome!

What makes it different is that it's 4-D (so you wear special glasses). Your ride vehicle spins into colorful rooms full of special effects and fun targets to shoot at. Pull the trigger on your blaster to "shoot" balls, darts, rings and other fun toys at the targets!

Your car holds four people (two on each side) and has an electronic scorecard that keeps track of your fancy shooting. Compete with others to see who can rack up the most points.

Throughout the ride, try to spot all your favorite Toy Story characters, including Buzz, Woody, Jessie, Rex and Hamm. They cheer you on!

This is a fun game for kids of all ages - it's even a favorite among Grandparents! Since it's one of the few attractions for any age at California Adventure, it's very popular. Get Lightning Lane reservations or visit early in the day to avoid waiting too long

Paradise Gardens Park

Paradise Gardens is located on the north side of the *bay*. (A bay is an inlet of water from an ocean or sea.)

Enjoy a nice rest during the day with a beautiful view of the water and Ferris wheel. You can even listen to a live band in the evening.

Paradise Gardens is often used for live entertainment, character meet and greets and special events such as the Lunar New Year.

Make sure to check the Disneyland app to see what events are taking place when you are in the parks.

Golden Zephyr

Back in the 1920s, fantastical tales of astronauts

and heroes sailing through outer space in shiny spaceships to save the world became very popular in science-fiction movies and story books.

Climb aboard a retro spaceship, inspired from these stories, and take a ride up in the sky. Close your eyes and imagine you are the pilot of your own rocket, as you soar around and around!

Goofy's Sky School

Hang on tight as you ride this Goofy roller coaster! This flight will take you up and down, it zigs and zags and dips. Earn your pilot wings by passing Goofy's Sky School.

This coaster is three stories high and has 1,200 feet of tracks. It's fast, but it ends quickly. This is a great first roller coaster if you've never ridden one before.

Do the silly scenes look familiar? The ride was inspired by Disney's "How to" cartoon called Goofy's Glider from 1940.

Jumpin' Jelly Fish

Swim on over to the Jumpin' Jelly Fish to float up 40 feet in the air. Just like a jelly fish, you slowly descend back down and then back up again!

This is a perfect starter ride to try first if you are worried about going on Guardians of the Galaxy – Mission: BREAKOUT! It will get you warmed up for that attraction's bigger drop.

Silly Symphony Swings

Whirl through the air on these silly swings. Just like the Silly Symphony cartoons, an orchestra plays during the action, as you get higher and higher. The songs get faster and faster, and the music gets louder and louder with this fun ride!

Silly Symphony Swings is a zany spin on the 1935 cartoon, "The Band Concert." Conductor Mickey Mouse must keep his orchestra playing as a tornado comes in and sweeps them up and lifts the whole orchestra in the sky.

The Little Mermaid ~ Ariel's Undersea Adventure

Journey underwater with Ariel and become part of her world. Step aboard your own "clam-mobile"—a giant clamshell and journey under the sea into Ariel's world!

This attraction contains a neat special effect that makes it seem like you're going under the sea, even though you don't actually get wet. There's a lot of amazing things to look at.

You can sing favorite songs and help battle the giant sea witch, Ursula! Look for your favorite friends, including Flounder and Sebastian.

Grizzly Peak

California doesn't just have palm trees, they actually have some of the tallest and oldest trees in America.

These forests are made up of Redwood and Sequoia tress and some of them are hundreds of years old.

Grizzly Peak is surrounded by forests, which highlights California's beautiful wilderness outdoor sports life.

If you need to cool off after a long, hot day *Grizzly River Run* is the perfect ride for you. You will get very wet! Warn your parents, so they can wear ponchos if they don't want to get soaking wet!

Head over to Grizzly Peak Airfield to ride *Soarin' Around the World* or take a picture with Pluto!

Grizzly River Run

Need to cool off in the intense California heat? You're bound to get soaked on Grizzly River Run!

This water raft ride starts out as a peaceful trip through the rain forest, but then gets fast and fun. Hold on tight as your raft drops over a huge waterfall!

Try to pay attention to your surroundings, while your raft bumps along the rocky sides and bobs up and down in the water. There's actually an important environmental message about deforestation you can easily miss while having fun.

While waiting in the queue (and briefly during the ride) you see how logging in the rain forests is having a devastating effect on the environment. (Logging is cutting down the trees for lumber, to make houses and buildings.)

You even see some timber (logs) burning and catch a waft (or smell) of real smoke!

Lots of people leave this ride completely soaked! You may think the drenching is over when you see the docking station up ahead, but there's still more fun to be had! Take note of the stone elephants near the end of the journey. People standing on the bridge use buttons to shoot water at you from the elephants' trunks. You can get in on the soaking action after you exit the ride!

It doesn't really matter where you sit in the raft. Every seat gets wet, while some get super drenched!

Even if a seat looks dry as you board, it just means the last person soaked all the water up on their clothes.

Have a towel and a spare set of clothes handy, including shoes and socks. Or wear a poncho with clothes that dry easily. Leave anything you need to keep dry (including electronics and your change of clothes) in a locker near the entrance. It is free to use for up to 2 hours, so there's no reason not to take advantage of it.

You probably won't need to change your clothes if you're visiting on a super hot day, though. The hot sun will dry you off pretty quickly.

Minimum Height Required: 38" tall (3 feet, 2 inches)

Redwood Creek

Give you parents a nice break while you go rock climbing and crawl around a huge outdoor jungle gym. Your parents can enjoy relaxing on one of the many benches in the shade while you play in the caves, swing on a tire swing and climb on the rope course!

The Spirit Caves will reveal to you what your true spirit animal is. Will your spirit animal be a wolf, bear or… stinky skunk!

Soarin' Around the World

Buckle up and away you go! In this attraction, guests are seated in a giant hang glider that holds many people. Soarin' is a unique ride that takes you on a simulated (meaning it seems real, but isn't) hang-gliding trip across the globe.

Fly high in the sky above the mountains and down low, nearly touching water as you view some of the most iconic sights in our world: pyramids, the Great Wall of China, the Eiffel Tower, Sydney, and more!

Your hang-gliding adventure ends as you finally return home to Disneyland.

Soarin' was filmed using special cameras mounted on airplanes and helicopters. It feels like you're really hang-gliding, tilting back and forth. There are even scents and breezes to convince you that you're flying during this five-minute ride!

Entertainment
World of Color

Every night at closing time is a huge water show with lasers, projectors, fire and awesome music. As classic Disney music booms over the loudspeakers, the crowd watches as Disney highlights characters from your favorite Disney movies. The show takes place in the middle of Paradise Bay, and you can see it from just about anywhere around the bay.

About the Show

Full-color laser systems shine from around the bay as projectors display patterns and images on the dancing water. Watch the bay become a water wonderland! It is a spectacular show and a perfect way to end your day at California Adventure.

Pin Trading

You can trade Disney pins with other guests or Cast Members throughout Disneyland and California Adventure. Take a couple of pins with you when you visit a park in case you want to make a trade! Make sure an adult is with you when you talk to anyone you don't know! Get permission for the pins you want to trade in case one of them is special to your parent or to your brother or sister!

Disney's Junior Dance Party

Boogie down on the dance floor with "Mickey and the Roadster Racers", " Doc McStuffins", "Vampirina", and "The Lion Guard" as the DJ plays all your favorite Disney Channel tunes! Sing and dance the night away!

Guardians of the Galaxy: Awesome Dance Off!

Who doesn't love to dance to Peter Quills playlist?! Watch and Gamora and Peter have a dance off with the crowd. Don't be afraid to them your best dance moves!

Avengers Assemble!

Watch the Avengers kick some real bad guy butt in Avengers Assemble. See Black Window and Black Panther flight bad guys on top of the Avengers Headquarters.

The Amazing Spider-Man!

This short stunt show is located on top of the WEB building. Watch as Spiderman hangs upside down and does stunts across the building to try out his new suit. The show features a one-of-a-kind robot that flies from one side of the building to the other. Can you spot the robotic Spiderman? Hint: for the best viewing spot of the show, sit across from the WEB building near the graffiti.

Operation: Playtime! Featuring the Green Army Patrol

Join the Green Army Men from Toy Story on the quest to find potential new recruits The Army Men travel in their jeep and by foot strumming their drums. Show them you've got what it takes to be an Army Man with your chanting skills!

Character Meet & Greets

There are a lot of places to meet characters at Disney's Hollywood Studios.

The Incredibles greet kids on Pixar Place, while Mickey and Minnie have a special location on the Red Carpet, just off of Commissary Lane. Nearby, Olaf is always celebrating summer near Echo Lake.

Chewbacca, **Kylo Ren** and **BB-8**, everyone's favorite droid, can be found in *Star Wars Launch Bay*. Just outside, meet **Disney Junior Pals** in the *Animation Courtyard*.

Meanwhile, **Buzz Lightyear**, **Woody** and their friends are on-hand to greet kids in the spectacular *Toy Story Land*.

Be sure to ask a Cast Member for a Guide Map and Times Guide to see who is there the day you visit.

Character	Location
Mickey Mouse, Minnie Mouse & Goofy	Buena Vista Street

TOP ATTRACTION RATINGS		
Super Cool (MUST-SEE)	**Cool (SHOULD SEE)**	**Fun (SEE IF YOU CAN)**
Goofy's Sky School	Animation Academy	Luigi's Rollickin' Roadsters
Grizzly River Run	Golden Zephyr	Redwood Creek Challenge Trail
Guardians of the Galaxy — Mission: BREAKOUT!	Inside Out Emotional Whirlwind	Sorcerer's Workshop
Incredicoaster	Jessie's Critter Carousel	The Bakery Tour
Pixar Pal Around	Jumpin' Jellyfish	Turtle Talk with Crush
Radiator Springs Racers	Mater's Junkyard Jamboree	
Soarin' Around the World	Mickey's PhilharMagic	
The Little Mermaid ~ Ariel's Undersea Adventure	Monster's, Inc. Mike & Sully to the Rescue!	
Toy Story Midway Mania!	Silly Symphony Swings	
WEB SLINGERS: A Spider-Man Adventure		

Other Fun Stuff at Disney (and Other Nearby Places)

You've already read through the sections on the theme parks, so you know all about the great shows and parades.

We've also mentioned a lot of the other fun things to do. Here are a few more things you can enjoy at Disneyland.

Special Park Tours

Every day at Disneyland is special, but there are ways to make it even more amazing.

Disney has lots of tours and special events available, which you can view at:

https://disneyland.disney.go.com/events-tours/

Most Disneyland tours are designed to be educational. If you're skipping out of school for your vacation, taking an educational tour might make your teacher really happy!

If your family has a different idea for a tour than the regular ones, you can hire a Disney expert to be your private tour guide. They can help you create a custom experience that's sure to be special.

These tours are called Disneyland Resort VIP Tours, because your whole family is treated like VIPs (Very Important Persons)!

If you decide you want a standard, educational tour, we include details about them below.

The Grand Circle Tour

Train lovers unite! You already know how much Walt Disney loved trains. How would you like to learn all about Disneyland's special railroad?

The Grand Circle Tour is a two-hour long event. A tour guide walks through the park with you and explains all the ways trains inspired Mr. Disney and his cartoons. You also get to ride in a very special parlor car on the Lily Belle train!

Wear sneakers and bring something to drink. The cost is $85 for each member of your party 3 years or older.

Ask a parent to call 714-781-TOUR (781-8687) for reservations.

Walk in Walt's Disneyland Footsteps Tour

Do you want to find out more about the man who dreamed up Disneyland?

This tour highlights Walt's history with the park. You get to go on some of the classic rides Mr. Disney helped design, while learning some cool facts. Lunch or dinner is included for you when the tour ends!

Ask a parent to call 714-781-TOUR (781-8687) to get the current price and reservations.

Disney Princess Breakfast Adventures

While it's not exactly a tour, breakfast with princesses is always a special experience!

Unlike other character dining experiences, this on includes storytime with some of your favorite princesses. It can't be beat!

This breakfast experience is pretty expensive. It's $125 per person (plus tax and tips). If you're celebrating a really special occasion and your parents want to make a reservation, ask a parent to make a reservation at https://disneyland.disney.go.com/dining/grand-californian-hotel/disney-princess-breakfast-adventures/.

Downtown Disney

https://disneyland.disney.go.com/destinations/downtown-disney-district/

Do you love shopping? How about eating? Who doesn't love getting thier groove on with live music and dance? Downtown Disney is *the* place to shop, eat, dance and play!

Much of Downtown Disney is in the process of being built brand new. There's always something new to discover!

Grab a fun milkshake from Black Tap Craft Burgers & Shakes or some delicious ice cream from Salt & Straw. If you arrive during one of Disney's famous festivals, such as the Food & Wine Festival, you can find some really good festival inspired foods at select locations.

If you love art, don't forget to stop into WonderGround Gallery to take a look at all the wonderful Disney paintings.

Also located in Downtown Disney is the Lego Store, where you can buy Lego sets or just build fun cities for FREE!

Entertainment

If you want a little more action, compete to see who is the best bowler at **Splitsville**, a two-story bowling alley. They serve really good food while you bowl!

Shopping

If you've got some money burning a hole in your pocket or super generous parents, Downtown Disney has some of the best shopping anywhere!

Star Wars Trading Post is out of this world. You can get all of your galactic gear there, including light sabers!

The other kid favorite in Downtown Disney is the **LEGO** store! That's right - LEGOS! You can even play there without having to buy anything!

Food

With all the shopping and playing around, you're bound to get hungry. There's practically a place to eat around every corner in Downtown Disney. Try **Ralph Brennan's Jazz Kitchen** for tasty cajun seafood and jazz music.

Kids really go wild for **La Brea Bakery Cafe**. The scent of freshly baking bread will have you drooling!

Disney Cruise Line
https://disneycruise.disney.go.com/

Want to go beyond the parks? Take a trip aboard a gigantic cruise ship with Mickey and all his friends!

You can sail to the Caribbean islands from San Diego, which is just a short drive from Disneyland. At each stop, there are plenty of places to play in the ocean, run and scream!

And the swimming pools! There are so many fun pools aboard each Disney Cruise ship — one even has a water coaster!

There are also adult-only pools… in case mom and dad want a break from you kids. Don't worry, though. Disney has the best kids-only stuff on their ships to give you a fun time away from your parents!

Fun Stuff Outside of Disney

Disneyland has so much neat stuff that you can have an entire vacation and never have to leave their property! But, just because you're going to Disney doesn't mean you can't find other fun things to do.

Remember, Los Angeles, California is the Entertainment Capital of the World! That means there are loads of cool activities around.

Here are some other fun things to do around California.

Los Angeles Area

Knott's Berry Farm

Disneyland may be the most famous theme park in the world, but it wasn't the first. Just down the road from Disneyland is the place that gets that credit: Knott's Berry Farm!

Knott's Berry Farm is just a short car ride away from Disneyland. Mrs. Knott started selling incredible fried chicken and yummy boysenberries at her farm. It wasn't long before this tiny farm turned into a 160 acre fun amusement park.

Fun Fact: At speeds of up to 56 mph, **GhostRider** is one of the longest and tallest wooden roller coasters in the world.

For you thrill seekers, **HangTime** is 150 feet tall and has a 96 Degree drop reaching speeds of 57mph!

Fun Fact: HangTime was the first dive coaster in California!

The **Xcelerator** will rocket you from 0-82 mph in 2.3 seconds up 205 feet into the air before immediately hurtling 90 degrees straight down!

On **Silver Bullet**, riders will spiral, corkscrew and fly into a cobra roll and a giant loop of 105 feet.

Some of those rides might sound intimidating and scary, but Knott's Berry Farm has a whole lot more than just scary thrill rides. There are lots of kids rides like a train, bumper cars, swings, merry-go-round and even a ferris wheel. You can watch a real-life blacksmith, ride on a horse-drawn stagecoach and even mine for gold!

Knott's Soak City

Soak City is 15 acres of water park fun, located just across the street from the Knott's Berry Farm!

Whether you like to play on the fun water slides, take a rest and float down the lazy river or play in the wave pool, this water park has a little bit for everyone.

Fun Fact: There's a three-story beach house. The splash zone has 200 water guns, nozzles, sprayers and other soggy surprises!

Universal Studios Hollywood

Universal Studios has a huge, amazing theme park in Hollywood, California. You can ride roller coasters, play with little yellow minions or find out what it's like to be a wizard at Universal Studios!

The theme park has different themed lands and super fun rides, much like Disney.

Hop on the **Transformers** Ride to help Optimus Prime protect the AllSpark from the Decepticons. Take a ride on the dark indoor roller coaster, the **Mummy**. (Watch out for ghosts!)

Best yet, you can find out what it's like to be a wizard like Harry Potter as you visit shops in Hogsmeade and go on a fantastic ride inside of Hogwarts School of Witchcraft and Wizardry!

When you're taking a break from the thrill rides, you can take a backlot tour and see where the movies are made!

Six Flags Magic Mountain

Magic Mountain may be the thrill capital of the World. If you are looking to try some record-breaking thrill rides, Six Flags is for you!

The Apocalypse is a huge, fast wooden roller coaster. Watch out for explosions as you zoom up and down!

Help fight crime in Gotham on the Batman ride. Brace yourself for a full 360-degree loop when you fly down this track If you love that, try New Revolution – it was the world's first 360-degree loop coaster.

For a different thrill, climb aboard Full Throttle, the fastest looping roller coaster in the world. Hop on Wonder Woman Flight of Courage next. It's the tallest and longest single-rail coaster on the planet.

There's always a debate with family and friends as to what type of roller coaster is better, wood or steel. You don't have to choose between the two at Magic Mountain. Check out the hybrid coaster Twisted Colossus - it contains both wood and steel tracks!

Don't worry if roller coasters aren't for you. Not everyone enjoys the thrill. just like other theme parks, this one has tame rides to enjoy.

Outside Los Angeles

Legoland

Legoland was built just for kids! It's great for anyone 12 and under, but especially great for those who love playing with Legos. Legoland has more than 60 rides, shows and attractions, along with over 5,000 sea creatures and a water park that takes up 10 acres!

Legoland's water park is called Chima Water Park. You can float down a lazy river on a Lego raft or try your hand at building with giant Lego blocks. Next, race family members down the **Twin Chasers** and **Riptide Racers** to see who can make it down the water slides the fastest!

At **Legoland's Sea Life Aquarium**, you can have an up-close encounter with sea creatures, including sharks, octopi and rays!

If you decide to stay overnight near Legoland, try one of the super cool Legoland Hotels: **Legoland Castle Hotel** or the **Legoland Hotel**. They have themed rooms. You can choose between Knights & Dragons, Royal Princess, Magic Wizard Pirate, Kingdom, Adventure, Lego Ninjago or Lego Friends. Wow!

These hotels have LEGO décor throughout, free breakfast, fun Lego play areas and they are both located at the main entrance of Legoland!

Fun Fact: California's 250-room Legoland Hotel was the nation's first LEGOLAND Hotel.

Sea World San Diego

Sea World San Diego is dedicated to all things related

to the ocean. While it has lots of rides, it is more than just a theme park.

This is where you can learn all about sea life. Meet whales, dolphins, sea lions, sharks and many more aquatic forms of life. Many of the animals perform in shows!

If that's not enough, visit the North Pole at the Penguin Encounter. You can also travel on a moving walkway through a clear acrylic tube inside a 600,000-gallon aquarium in the "Sharks!" pavilion.

Of course, theme parks need rides. There are some great ones at Sea World, including *Manta* (named after the Manta rays) and *Electric Eel*, the tallest and fastest roller coaster in all of San Diego!

Want some more adventure? You can swim with dolphins or beluga whales, dine with Orcas (killer whales) or have an up-close encounter with penguins and sea lions!

Long Beach

If you have never been to the ocean before, Long Beach is not far from Anaheim (where Disneyland is located). Take the short drive to the beach and see the historic Queen Mary. It's a first-class cruise ship from the 1930s. You can also rent some bicycles or just relax on the beach and count the container ships.

The water is cold and refreshing. Take a dip in the ocean but be sure to have your beach towel handy!

Other Neat Attractions

Less than one-hour from Disneyland, you can reach **Medieval Times** (dinner and a show), **Pirates Dinner and Adventure** (dinner and a show), Flightdeck Simulator (learn how to fly a plane) and the **Great Wolf Lodge** (indoor water park).

Just another 30 minutes away and you can see **Sequoia National Park** (the tallest and oldest trees in the USA). The trees are so big, you can drive a car through them!

Color Oga's Cantina!

Kid Favorite Character Buffets
(Meet Characters While You Eat!)

Disney Princess Breakfast Adventures	Napa Rose, Grand California Hotel (Breakfast Only)
Goofy's Kitchen	Disneyland Hotel
Mickey's Tales of Adventure	Storytellers Café, Grand Californian Hotel (Breakfast & Weekend Brunch Only)

Disney has plenty of healthy and delicious choices for kids. Look for this symbol at food service establishments to know what is especially yummy and healthy for you:

Are you a budding foodie? Get ready to blog about your favorite Disney eats!

There are more places to find food than you can imagine. A lot of the food is stuff you've tried before, like burgers and pizzas.

If you look around, though, there are very different flavors than you may have encountered. Some of them have very strong spices and unique tastes.

If you don't like surprises, don't worry! Most restaurants have a special menu just for kids. Just ask the server! If you're not checking carbs, here are some favorite meal and snack options and locations where you can find them. The tasty treats on this list should satisfy the appetite of any kid:

Disneyland Park

Restaurant (Location)	Food Type
Sweets	
Gibson Girl Ice Cream Parlor (Main Street USA)	Ice Cream
Maurice's Treats (Fantasyland)	Frozen Slushies, Donut Holes
Milk Stand (Star Wars Galaxy's Edge)	Blue & Green (Alien!) Milk
Olga's Cantina (Star Wars Galaxy's Edge)	Fun, Fruity Slushies
Tiki Juice Bar (Adventureland)	Pineapple Dole Whip
Tropical Hideaway (Adventureland)	Dole Whip (Multiple Flavors)
Snacks	
Churro Carts (Multiple Locations)	Churros
Jolly Holiday Bakery Café (Main Street USA)	Macarons, Cookies, Muffins

Restaurant (Location)	Food Type
Popcorn Carts (Multiple Locations)	Popcorn
Pretzel Carts (Multiple Locations)	Mickey Pretzels
Turkey Leg Carts (Multiple Locations)	Giant Turkey Legs
Meals	
Alien Pizza Planet (Tomorrowland)	Pizza
Blue Bayou (New Orleans Square)	Chicken & Pasta
Docking Bay 7 Food and Cargo (Star Wars Galaxy's Edge)	Chicken Tenders & Mac 'n Cheese
Galactic Grill (Tomorrowland)	Burgers & Mac 'n Cheese
Minnie and Friends - Breakfast in the Park, Plaza Inn (Main Street USA)	Breakfast Buffet
Red Rose Tavern (Fantasyland)	Chicken Tenders, Burgers & Flatbread
The Golden Horseshoe (Frontierland)	Chicken Tenders

California Adventure

Restaurant (Location)	Food Type
Sweets	
Adorable Snowman Frosted Treats (Pixar Pier)	Soft Serve Ice Cream
Clarabelle's Hand-Scooped Ice Cream (Buena Vista Street)	Ice Cream
Ghirardelli Soda Fountain and Chocolate Shop (Pacific Wharf)	Ice Cream & Chocolates

Jack-Jack Cookie Num Nums (Pixar Pier)	Cookies
Schmoozies! (Hollywood Land)	Ice Cream
Snacks	
Churro Carts (Multiple Locations)	Churros
Popcorn Carts (Multiple Locations)	Popcorn
Pretzel Carts (Multiple Locations)	Mickey Pretzels
Senior Buzz Churros (Pixar Pier)	Churros
Terran Treats (Avengers Campus)	Pastries
Turkey Leg Carts (Multiple Locations)	Giant Turkey Legs
Meals	
Corn Dog Castle (Paradise Garden Park)	Corn Dogs
Cozy Cone Motel (Cars Land)	Chili; Mac 'n Cheese Cones
Flo's V8 Café (Cars Land)	Chicken Tenders & Mac 'n Cheese
Lucky Fortune Cookery	Burritos; Teriyako Chicken
Poultry Palace (Pixar Pier)	Chicken Drumsticks; Giant Turkey Legs
Pym Test Kitchen (Avengers Campus)	Peanut Butter & Jelly Sandwiches; Pasta & Meatballs

Downtown Disney

Restaurant	Food Type
Sweets	
Crazy Shake Window by Black Tap	Specialty Milkshakes
Jamba	Smoothies
Salt & Straw	Ice Cream
Sprinkles	Cupcakes
Snacks	
Wetzels Pretzels	Specialty Pretzels
Meals	
Ralph Brennan's Jazz Kitchen	Chicken Tenders; Burgers; Pasta & Meatballs
Splitsville	Burgers; Pizza
Tortilla Joes	Burritos; Tacos; Quesadillas

Food Allergies

If you, or someone in your family, has food allergies, you can ask for an Allergy Friendly menu at every Quick Service location. You can order from that menu, or even ask to speak to a manager who will help you make safe, allergy-free food choices.

Hotel Dining

There's plenty of *nosh* (food) at the Disney hotels! Keep in mind - while all of the restaurants located inside the parks allow for "park casual dress," the dress code for certain Resort Restaurants may call for you to dress up a bit nicer!

Dinner reservations are usually required at the hotel, so have an adult book early on the Disneyland app or through the disneyland.disney.go.com/dining/ website!

Character Dining
disneyland.disney.go.com/dining/#/character-dining/

Character Dining is a big deal. It's a great way to meet Mickey and the gang, your favorite princesses and more without the wait - they come to meet you!

While there are character restaurants inside the parks, you might find it's even better to attend character meals at the hotels!

Try to do it on a day you don't plan to go to the parks. Your family has a more relaxed time because you're not rushed to get back to rides.

Chef Goofy presides over his namesake restaurant at the Disneyland Hotel. This is one of the most popular spots for meeting characters and getting a great meal!

Dinner Show

The Disney Princess Breakfast Adventure takes character dining to a whole other level - and kids love it!

Listen to your favorite princesses tell a story, while you enjoy a tasty meal!

This dinner show is held at in the Grand Californian Hotel, which is also a really cool place to visit and just have a look around.

Find the Disney Princesses

```
N B L A A L M U N N A B U R
H E T A U R T L W P E N P L
U A I R R E L S R S I A O R
R A A I O A I E A I L L C N
A B N L R S N N D L E U A A
P E A A A I N C E D R M H R
U L P A N A M R A L D R O L
N L E R E I E M O A N A N O
Z E M I E D I R N R H T T I
E U E N N M L U A P N A A E
L L E I J A S M I N E J S N
J J C L I O A R I E L N N B
N E T I H W W O N S A A A E
I I A D I R E M R T M O A E
```

AURORA
ARIEL
CINDERELLA
SNOW WHITE
JASMINE
MULAN
TIANA
MERIDA
POCAHONTAS
BELLE
MOANA
RAPUNZEL

Let's Eat at Disneyland!

Let's Stay at a Disney Hotel!

Color Disneyland Hotel!

Disneyland Resorts (Hotels)

Disney calls its hotels *resorts*, because there is so much to do at each of the 3 Disney-owned ones they have next to Disneyland.

Each properties has its own, unique theme

What do we mean by themes? Think of it this way: one property transports you to classic Californian boardwalks, while another takes you to the rustic wilderness!

Each hotel has different amenities and price ranges to match your family's size and unique needs.

All of the resorts have great pools, water slides and hot tubs to soak in after walking around all day.

Kid's Tip!

Remember to drink lots of water and don't forget to apply sunscreen often. It's especially easy to forget when you're playing in the water, and you're more likely to get a nasty sunburn at a pool. Ouch!

Plus, each hotel is within easy walking distance to the parks and Downtown Disney!

The most affordable Disney hotel is **Paradise Pier**. It's designed to make you feel as though you're staying at the beach, complete with a boardwalk.

> **Did you know?** Boardwalks get their names because the path is made from actual wooden planks!

While the pool isn't as neat as the other Disney hotels, it's located on the roof of a very tall building. That makes it a lot of fun.

Disney's mid-priced hotel is the classic **Disneyland Hotel**. The Disneyland Hotel was built way back in 1955. That's the same year Disneyland Park was built!

That doesn't mean the hotel looks old, though. It gets lots of upgrades all the time and is one of the nicest hotels around the parks.

This is a kid-favorite place to stay. It has different themed areas just like Disneyland, including a fantasy, adventure and even a frontier area!

The reason kids love the Disneyland Hotel the most, though, is the pool. The main pool includes a water play zone, plus two super-fun waterslides that look like monorails.

You may not want to go to the parks when you realize how much fun it is to play at the hotel!

The third Disney hotel is the most expensive: **Grand Californian Hotel & Spa**.

If you're into luxury, artwork and fun details to discover, this is the place for your family.

You may think you're in a mountain-top lodge when you step through the doors of this hotel. Wood carvings and beams are everywhere.

Step out the back door, though, and discover you're actually at Disney's California Adventure Park. The hotel has its own, private entrance!

Did we mention the Grand Californian has a spa? Talk about pampering. Your parents can treat themselves to a massage, while you play at one of the three pools!

If you're into fitness, all the Disney resorts have gyms, though who needs the extra exercise with all of the walking around the parks?

Some families want to splurge on a once-in-a-lifetime vacation, while others return year-after-year and want to stay on a strict budget. No matter which resort you choose, you can be assured there will be tons of fun and frolicking.

Disney imagineers came up with amazing designs and details for each resort, and every one has a very cool swimming pool (or three)!

Staying on Disney property keeps you just a few minutes away from all the action. This is because all Disney resorts are a short walk to the parks, Downtown Disney and the monorail station.

Even if you are staying at one resort, you can visit any of the others to check them out, eat a meal or just explore!

Forget the alarm clock. Have your parents call the front desk to schedule a wake-up call for an early-morning phone call directly from one of the characters.

It might be Mickey Mouse, but if he is busy, he might ask Stitch or another buddy to make the call.

> **Kid's Tip!**
>
> Watch the tourist channel on Disney Resort TV. It shows an exciting preview of some of the amazing fun you can find throughout Disneyland.

Disney is like Alice stepping through the looking glass; to step through the portals of Disney will be like entering another world.

- Walt Disney

Disney Villains

Across
1. Tik Tok the crocodile ate Captain _____'s hand.
4. This sea witch wants King Triton's power.
7. She wants to make a coat from 101 Dalmatians.
9. Mufasa's jealous brother from The Lion King.
10. This man plots dastardly deeds against Belle's father, Maurice.

Down
1. No bug's life show would be complete without this nasty grasshopper.
2. Don't forget to invite this wicked fairy to your party.
3. Lady _____ is Cinderella's wicked stepmother.
5. Alice must outwit the Queen of _____.
6. Who holds power over Agrabah with a snake staff?
8. The _____ Queen was the original Disney villain.

*Answers on Page 156

Puzzle Answers

Did you enjoy the puzzles in this book? We hope you solved all of them! If you need a little help, here are the answers to the crossword puzzles.

Disney Princesses

Across
2. Don't mess with this princess who has been to war. <u>Mulan</u>
4. <u>Snow</u> White was the first Disney princess.
5. This princess dreams of a life on land. <u>Ariel</u>
7. She knows how to get down and dirty with a mop. <u>Cinderella</u>
9. Don't cut her really long hair! <u>Rapunzel</u>

Down
1. She'll make you see the "Colors of the Wind." <u>Pocahontas</u>
3. The sea called out to this princess. <u>Moana</u>
5. She met her true love and prince, before she even knew she was a princess. <u>Aurora</u>
6. The only way to her heart is through a library. <u>Belle</u>
8. Only her sister, the Queen, could save her from a cold spell. <u>Anna</u>

Disney Trivia

Across
3. The first name of Walt Disney's older brother and partner. <u>Roy</u>
5. Mickey Mouse's lady friend. <u>Minnie</u>
6. In which state is Disneyland located? <u>California</u>
8. April, May & <u>June</u> are the names of Daisy's nieces.
9. In what month was Walt Disney born? <u>December</u>

Down
1. Who was Walt Disney's favorite president? <u>Lincoln</u>
2. Walt considered this Missouri city to be his home town. <u>Marceline</u>
4. A lucky rabbit. <u>Oswald</u>
7. The first Disney theme park to open. <u>Disneyland</u>
8. In what month did Disneyland open? <u>June</u>

Disney Villains

Across
1. Tik Tok the crocodile ate Captain <u>Hook</u>'s hand.
4. This sea witch wants King Triton's power. <u>Ursula</u>
7. She wants to make a coat from 101 Dalmatians. <u>Cruella</u>
9. Mufasa's jealous brother from The Lion King. <u>Scar</u>
10. This man plots dastardly deeds against Belle's father, Maurice. <u>Gaston</u>

Down
1. No bug's life show would be complete without this nasty grasshopper. <u>Hopper</u>
2. Don't forget to invite this wicked fairy to your party. <u>Maleficent</u>
3. Lady <u>Tremaine</u> is Cinderella's wicked stepmother.
5. Alice must outwit the Queen of <u>Hearts</u>.
6. Who holds power over Agrabah with a snake staff? <u>Jafar</u>
8. The <u>Evil</u> Queen was the original Disney villain.

Thank you for purchasing this guidebook. We appreciate our readers and value your support, as we strive for excellence in our materials.

If you enjoy our book, please have your parents **rate or review** it.

Like and follow **Disney Made *Easy*** on Facebook:

www.facebook.com/groups/DisneyMadeEasyWDW

Share your love of Disney with us by joining our Facebook group:

Mickey's Not So Secret Disney Fan Group

www.facebook.com/groups/mickeysfangroup

Made in the USA
Monee, IL
02 October 2024

67013358R00095